ZEBULON VANCE, TARHEEL SPOKESMAN

BY

FRANKLIN RAY SHIRLEY

McNALLY AND LOFTIN, *Publishers*
Charlotte / Santa Barbara

Printed in the United States of America
Heritage Printers, Inc.
Charlotte, N. C.

To My Wife
and Children

PREFACE

Perhaps in all of North Carolina's history no name has been more revered by the people of the state than that of Zebulon Baird Vance. Yet, in spite of the deep admiration by the people, scholars have been extremely reticent in presenting a systematic study of any phase of his life. Since his effectiveness as a politician, statesman, and leader of his people may be directly attributed to his oratorical powers, a full length critical treatment of his public speaking appears long overdue.

It is the intent of this book to compensate for this apparent neglect of Vance by historians, biographers, and rhetorical critics, by providing a chronological view of his public speaking with an analysis and evaluation of its effectiveness.

In fulfillment of this purpose, the author is indebted to many individuals for inspiration and guidance. Among these is the late Professor Dallas C. Dickey of the University of Florida, who stimulated interest in this undertaking. Without his suggestions and criticisms during the formative stages of the study, it probably would have never materialized. A major debt of gratitude is owed to Professor H. P. Constans of the University of Florida. His frank and generous suggestions have contributed greatly to the fruition of the work. Professor Douglas W. Ehninger of the State University of Iowa also deserves commendation for his willingness to give freely of his time and editorial experience. The writer is indebted to the late Professor James D. Glunt of the University of Florida whose teachings provided background knowledge essential to the work, and likewise to Professor George C. Osborne also of the University of Florida.

Several sources deserve credit for assistance in securing materials and aiding in research. Mrs. Mary Rogers and other members of the staff of the North Carolina Department of Archives and History were especially helpful in making the Vance Papers and other pertinent collections available. Mrs. Margaret Price of the North Carolina State Library provided invaluable assistance in locating newspaper sources used extensively throughout the study. Among the libraries and archives that made available material for the research were the Wake

Forest College Library, the University of North Carolina Library, Duke University Library, the University of Florida Library, the Moravian Archives of Winston-Salem, North Carolina, the Boston Public Library, the Atlanta Public Library, and the Library of Congress. Special thanks are due to the staff members of the Wake Forest College Library for their cooperation in supplying the majority of the secondary sources.

Several people are indirectly responsible for the completion of this project. Of these, the writer's wife, Mamie M. Shirley, deserves highest praise for the numerous sacrifices made while the study was in progress. His children, Susan Ollene, William McNulty, and Elizabeth Rae, have been helpful through their willingness to forego their father's companionship in anticipation of his completion of the book. The writer would be ungrateful, indeed, if he did not express appreciation to his father and his mother, Mr. and Mrs. W. F. Shirley, for their sacrifices in helping him to become equipped for this endeavor.

F. R. S.

Wake Forest College
Winston-Salem, North Carolina
August, 1962

CONTENTS

ZEBULON VANCE,
TARHEEL SPOKESMAN

CHAPTER I

BACKGROUND AND TRAINING

"I have another son . . . I call him Zebulon Baird. . . ."[1] These words, written by the child's mother to a relative, represent the only publicity given to the birth of the boy who was destined to become immortal in the hearts of the people of his state. Zebulon Baird Vance was born May 13, 1830, in the family home on Reems Creek, near the French Broad River in Buncombe County, North Carolina. He was the third son among the eight children of David and Mira Vance.[2]

The house had been built by Zebulon's grandfather, Colonel David Vance, who had come into the Reems Creek Valley in 1785.[3]

Few North Carolinians could boast a better lineage than Zebulon Baird Vance. The Vance family known originally as DeVaux, moved to England from Normandy. In England the name was shortened to Vaux, and later in Scotland it became Vans;[4] in 1660, in Ireland, it was altered to Vance.[5]

During the early part of the eighteenth century some of the Vance family came to America. David Vance, Zebulon's grandfather, was one of the descendants of these Scotch-Irish settlers. He was born in Frederick County, Virginia, in 1745, and settled in the Quaker Meadows section of the Catawba Valley in North Carolina when he was about twenty years old.[6] Vance, a surveyor and teacher, was one of the first to take up arms during the American Revolution.[7] David served under Colonel Charles Mc-Dowell, who led the Burke and Rutherford county militia against Major Patrick Ferguson's Loyalist force at King's Mountain. The total destruction of this British army has been called the "turn of the tide of success which terminated the Revolutionary War."[8]

1

Zebulon Vance's maternal grandfather, Zebulon Baird, was born in New Jersey in 1764. In 1775, his widowed mother moved with her three sons from Newark, New Jersey, to Burke County, North Carolina.[9] After their mother's death, the three Baird sons, Zebulon, Elisha, and Bedent, moved to Buncombe County and settled on the site of the city of Asheville. Zebulon married Hannah Early, whose Scotch-Irish family lived in nearby Burke County. Among the eight children born to the Bairds was Mira Margaret, who was to become the mother of Zebulon Baird Vance.[10]

Young Vance inherited little more than intelligence and good character from his father.[11] He was said to have received his wit, his love of nature, and his personality from his mother. At night she gathered the children around her and read aloud selections from the Bible, Shakespeare, or *Pilgrim's Progress*.[12] This daily practice contributed to Vance's store of literary and scriptural quotations which he later used in his speeches.

Zeb's early education was pursued in a random manner that contributed little to his moral or mental development. He was about six years old when he went to his first school at Flat Creek, twelve miles from his home. Then, for seven years Zeb attended first one and then another of the "old field" schools in his area. These served as kindergartens, graded, and normal schools.[13] Usually there were one or two such schools in each county, with sessions running when it was not crop-time. They were attended by people of all ages, with as many as a hundred pupils jammed into one room. Reading, writing, arithmetic, and spelling were the principal subjects taught. These schools were financed by public subscription, with the teacher receiving free board in the homes of the pupils.[14]

In 1843, when Zeb was thirteen years old, his father sent him across the mountains to Washington College in Jonesboro, Tennessee. Because of his meager early training, young Vance presumably enrolled for the preparatory program rather than the freshman course. His education was to follow a classical pattern.

Washington College was the seat of classical learning, serving eastern Tennessee and western North Carolina. Even in the preparatory course a student was required to study English grammar, geography, and Latin. Here, too, there was formal speech training, since a student was required to declaim, as well as to write compositions, once every four weeks.

Before young Vance had been at Washington College a year, his father died; at 14 he had to leave the school. But his mother was determined that her children should have the benefit of an education. With this end in view, she bought a house in Asheville. She put all the children in school, and played the chief role in directing their studies.

The only speech training received during this stage of Vance's education was probably provided by his mother. Vance once said, "She was the most correct and impressive reader I have ever heard off stage; and I am satisfied that whatever of elocution I have came from her."[15]

Inspired by his mother, Zeb became an avid reader. He made good use of his Uncle Robert's library, which had come into the possession of his family after his uncle's death. The library contained about five hundred volumes of the best literature, and included the works of Hume, Livy, Tacitus, Cicero, Scott, Swift, Addison, Pope, Byron, Shakespeare, and Milton. Among the available books, Smith's *Wealth of Nations* was of special interest to Zebulon. These books made a great impression on him, and some of his associates attributed his vigorous style of speaking to his reading.[16]

Vance retained much of what he read, and demonstrated a familiarity with the Bible, Shakespeare, and Scott's novels that enhanced his speaking throughout his illustrious career.

While still a boy, Vance resolved to set a high goal in life. One night John C. Calhoun, who was spending the summer in the North Carolina mountains, stopped at Zeb's home for the night. Calhoun became interested in the boy and invited him to go for a walk. Zeb was much impressed by the picture Calhoun drew of what he might become if he would cultivate his mind and apply himself to study. This may have been the stimulus that sparked his ambition; at any rate, from this point on, he became more concerned with his studies. For a time Zeb worked as a hotel clerk in order to earn enough money to continue his education.

In 1851, Vance, who was then living in Asheville, began private study in the law office of John W. Woodfin. In Woodfin's office he was a fellow student of August S. Merrimon, who later became chief justice of North Carolina. It became practically impossible, however, for him to concentrate on his studies while living in Asheville. The temptation to fish and swim was too overpowering, and he was unable to free himself from the village loafers who enjoyed Zeb's company more than they were sympathetic with his ambitions.[17]

In the summer of 1851, President David L. Swain of the University of North Carolina, who once considered Zeb's mother his sweetheart, received a letter from her son. Vance explained to Swain, who was called Governor by all who knew him, that his property was not very productive and he needed money with which to enter the university. Swain, a native of Buncombe County and a friend of the boy's family, willingly granted him a loan of $300 which enabled him to take a partial course in the university while pursuing his legal studies in the law school.[18]

Zeb arrived at Chapel Hill wearing ill-fitting clothes spun from his mother's loom. His sturdy ankles showed where his pants lacked about three inches of meeting his shoes. He was described by one who saw him for the first time as a "raw, gawky, awkward, ornery, ganglin [sic] sort of looking customer." Although he was not handsome, he had an elegant head of black hair, and his grayish deepset eyes were expressive.[19]

At the time Vance entered the university, it had a student body of 251, and a faculty of twelve. He pursued a course of study designed to prepare him, as quickly as possible, for the practice of law. Consequently, he enrolled as an "optional student" rather than a regular one.[20] In marked contrast to his old desultory habits of study he applied himself diligently, and commented on this in writing to his cousin, "Indeed you would hardly believe that I had taken to tremendous hard study, would you? It's the fact notwithstanding. I rise at 5 and go to bed at 10 and . . . don't lose more than two hours during that time and that is necessary for recreation."[21]

Instruction in constitutional law, intellectual philosophy, and moral science consumed three hours each week for the term of nine months. The question and answer method of recitation was used, with the teacher following the textbook very closely. Swain's course in national law served to sharpen Vance's keen memory, since he required his students to memorize the table of contents along with the marginal topics. It also instilled in him an interest in the great documents of government.

The law school was only nominally a department of the university. Judge William H. Battle, the professor of law, received no salary from the university and spent about half of his time away from his classes holding court. In his absence, the classes were taught by Samuel F. Phillips, a practicing lawyer.[22]

In order to give the students further practical training, the law professors conducted moot court sessions in which the students spoke on such legal questions as the professors might propose.[23] Vance distinguished himself as a speaker during at least one of these moot court trials when he was selected to conduct the defense of the "College Bore." The boy who bore this title had become a common nuisance because he wouldn't study, and spent most of his time keeping others from doing so. Vance's speech in the trial, it is said, not only teemed with wit and humor, but exhibited good reasoning in his "not guilty" plea. Employing the argument that Seargent S. Prentiss once used in defense of the bed-bug, he argued an analogy that the bore like the bed-bug was walking the path which the God of Nature had laid out for him and, in an explicable way, was serving his creator. The bore was designed to prepare his fellow men for Heaven by teaching them patience and fortitude while undergoing affliction.[24]

The Dialectic Literary Society offered another avenue of training to Vance during his year at the university. Here he gained practice in parliamentary law, in extempore speaking, and in the writing of compositions. Much that was not available in textbooks was learned in the society. Chiefly, Vance discovered his ability to be a leader and to become an effective debater. His strong, accurate memory, along with an easy command of words, made him one of the ablest debaters in the group. At the same time, his inimitable wit and humor served to replenish the treasury of the Dialectic Society. A fine was levied for every offense of audible laughter, and there were few who could resist laughing when Zeb spoke.[25]

Although he passed the examination for a license to practice in the county courts in December, 1851, Vance remained at Chapel Hill until the following May. Then, with his license in his pocket, he journeyed back to Asheville where he opened his office.

Vance became a lawyer in the western counties, and on horseback rode the circuit to serve the mountain area. Of his early law practice, he said later in a speech at the Law College of the District of Columbia, "I went out to court horseback and carried a pair of saddle-bags, with a change of shirts and the North Carolina Form-book in one end of the saddle bags, and it is none of your business what was in the other."[26]

Vance, in his year at Chapel Hill, enjoyed associating with the young women whom he met there, but reserved his love for a girl from his native mountains. On August 3, 1853, the day after he received his superior court license, he was married to his mountain sweetheart, Harriet Espy.[27]

Four sons — David, Charles, Zebulon, and Thomas — were born to the Vances, and if Zeb had any fault as a father, it was indulgence toward his children. His wife instilled in him a deep and abiding respect for religion, and, although he was not a professing Christian until after her death, he was interested in religion, believed in the Bible, and held to the Calvinistic system of theology. Because she was more rigorous in her notions of propriety than her husband, she found it difficult to condone his habitual use of coarse humor. Vance often spoke to his intimate friends of the restraining influence of his "little red-headed Presbyterian wife."[28]

Although law appeared to hold a promising future for Vance, he was by nature a politician. He liked people and people liked him, and he aspired to leadership. He was to find the opportunity for the development of his natural talents not in the courtroom but in the political arena.

CHAPTER II

YOUTHFUL POLITICIAN AND LAWMAKER

Vance's interest in politics manifested itself early in life; when only fourteen years of age, he wrote of the national political campaign of 1844:

I headed a procession on mule back ... marched sixteen miles to the election precinct through the mountains of Madison County, filled with patriotism, zeal for the Whig cause, and hard cider.... Ffteen separate and distinct fights were then and there had, in part of which I participated and for all of which I might be set down as the proximate cause.[1]

Several reasons explain why Vance turned from the practice of law to a career in politics. First, he felt his strength lay in politics rather than law. He amusingly told of the first compliment that he received for his forensic efforts: "Zeb," the mountaineer said, "if you can only get past the judge, I'd as lief have you as any old lawyer."[2] Although the people had as much confidence in him as in the older lawyers of the area, his knowledge of law was too limited. Once in the Madison County Court, Vance cited an opinion of the State Supreme Court to support his position in a case on trial. He did not once mention a recent act of the state legislature which had repealed that law. A. S. Merrimon, the opposition lawyer, rose with a volume of laws in his hand and read the repealing act. In turn, Vance sarcastically asked, "Gentlemen of the jury, are you not amazed at the assurance of my friend, Mr. Merrimon, in citing an act of the legislature, passed by such men as your good neighbor, John Smith, who knows no more law than you do and Bill Jones of Yancey, who knows less, against the decision of our Supreme Court constituted of such men as Ruffin, Gaston, and Daniel?" The ethics of such tactics might be questioned, but the incident showed his ability to pull himself from a hopeless and sudden dilemma produced by the lack of legal knowledge.[3] Such ability was an asset as a politician, but not a substitute for the skill required of a lawyer.

Vance's popularity and gifts as a stump speaker fitted him for his role in politics.[4] In the use of wit, broad humor, quick repartee, and boisterous eloquence, he was unsurpassed.[5] Such methods, calculated to win the unlettered farmers of his mountain district, meant that Vance never lacked a following. To be a leader of his people held more charm for Vance than did all the honors of law. He became a candidate for the lower house of the legislature, known then as the House of Commons.[6] This was in 1854, although he had tasted political victory a year before by means other than a vote of the people. In 1853, the magistrates of Buncombe County had shown their confidence in the young lawyer's ability and elected him to the office of county solicitor. Although the office was a minor one, his selection over A. S. Merrimon, who later became chief justice of the Supreme Court,[7] demonstrated his power to win men to his favor. To secure his seat in the legislature, Vance, "a regular built old fashioned Whig," entered his first race.[8]

As was true of all North Carolina Whigs, he belonged to the National Republican, internal improvement wing rather than the southern States Rights faction.[9]

Vance's campaign for the House of Commons lasted three months, and was a typical one in which the Whig and Democratic candidates indulged in "personal abuse, violent partisanship and petty bickering."[10] His opponent, a Colonel Reynolds,[11] was twice his age and a man of high standing in Buncombe County.[12] Vance, only twenty-four years old, was not expected to win. At the first public meeting of the two men in Asheville, the older candidate made fun of the beardless youth who wanted his seat in the legislature. When Vance's turn to speak came, he replied, "Fellow

Citizens, I admit I am young; but it is not my fault. My parents did not consult me as to the time when I should be born. All I can do is to promise to try to do better next time." This reply pleased the crowd, and his opponent never referred to his youth again. Vance won the election by 110 votes.

As a member of the 1854 legislature, Vance tended to show immaturity. At one time, for example, a fellow member offered a resolution dealing with the hours of meeting. Vance objected to the proposal by hissing the speaker. The speaker demanded to know the meaning of the hiss, and asked Vance to state whether it was intended as a personal insult to the author of the resolution, or if it merely represented disapproval of the proposition. Vance admitted that he had hissed; not to insult the speaker, however, but to show his contempt for the speaker's idea of remaining in session until nine o'clock without any supper.[13] Such tactics were hardly calculated to win him friends and to enhance his prestige.

Nevertheless, his experience in the legislature made him better known to his own constituents, and to the entire state. Vance became a candidate for the state senate from Buncombe County but was defeated. The defeat did not discourage Vance's political endeavors, for in 1857 he became a Whig candidate for the House of Representatives. Again he was defeated; apparently the disorganization of the Whig Party was responsible for this defeat. In 1858 he tried again, against a field of three other candidates. By this time, Vance was a more experienced politician. He was primed to carry on a heated campaign against his opponents, and his peculiar and unique powers as a politician and stump speaker rapidly developed in this contest. People applauded his gallantry, but laughed at his folly when he announced his intention of running for Congress.[14] Even his own family did not think he had a chance to win. One of his uncles told Richard H. Battle, "Zeb is a fool for running for Congress. He is getting a pretty good practice in law, and is throwing it all away, running for Congress, with no more chance of being elected than I have."[15]

The campaign was strenuous, taking the candidates into fifteen counties on a speaking tour that "set the mountains on fire."[16] At

Waynesville, Vance optimistically declared that he would win by three or four thousand votes if the Whigs would do their part. His opponent, Avery, then resurrected some of Vance's old articles in which he had denounced both the Whig and the Democratic parties as rotten and corrupt. He accused Vance of having written that the salvation of the country depended on the people joining the Know-Nothing party and fighting against the Pope and "furriners." Vance, in turn, replied that the Know-Nothing party was dead and that his opponent should let it rest.[17]

Just as politicians today use the hill-billy band and singing to secure a popular following, Vance used his fiddle. One day when he and Avery were scheduled to speak at a cross-roads, Vance was not present at the announced hour. Soon he arrived with a crowd of men leaping and dancing around him as he played the fiddle. Although Avery questioned the dignity of this episode, he could not doubt its effectiveness.

In political debate, as in forensic practice, Vance was none too ethical. During one discussion, Avery pictured him as representing a dying party with its leaders and sons of its leaders deserting it. He gave as examples the sons of Henry Clay and Daniel Webster. Thinking that Webster had only daughters, Vance promptly responded, "Daniel Webster has no sons, his children are all daughters." "Is it possible you do not remember Colonel Fletcher Webster of the Mexican War?" replied Avery. Vance, realizing his error, said that was "Noah Webster's son, the spelling-book man's son!" The audience went wild with delight, and Avery despaired of clarifying the matter. As he left the stand, he said, "Vance, that was a mean trick." To this Vance replied, "I know it was, Avery, but you had me so fast I had to wriggle out somehow."[18]

Everywhere in their joint canvass, Avery had said that Vance would stand no show for he could not overcome the Democratic majority of two thousand. To win the election by 2,049 votes[19] was a great victory for the young Whig. According to custom, a joint meeting of the two candidates was held after the election at Asheville to declare friendship and to heal old wounds. Vance made the most of his success as he told the audience:

My opponent charged that I would be snowed under, but was vice versa. I remind myself of the Caldwell County 'possum, which an indignant mountaineer told me about. Said he, I stretched that 'possum's neck tell [*sic*] I thought he was dead; I skinned him and biled him for three hours, but don't you think when I took the lid off'n the pot, the cussed little devil was settin' up there on its hind legs, and had licked up the gravy.[20]

At the age of twenty-eight, Vance became a member of the second session of the thirty-fifth Congress.[21] His first session was relatively quiet.[22]

Soon after the first of the year, however, he made his first speech when he introduced a motion to strike out the portion of the appropriations bill providing $40,000 for miscellaneous items.

Humor, in the form of an analogy, comprised the peroration of his brief speech. The House was thrown into laughter when he said, "This whole bill reminds me very much of the bills I have seen of fast young men at fashionable hotels — for two days board, five dollars, sundries, fifty dollars."

This first speech broke Vance's silence; three days later, on February 7, he spoke again. His second speech and the only one of any consequence which he gave during his first term in Congress, encompassed the subject of the tariff, public lands, and pensions for war veterans. Delivered while the House was in committee of the whole, Vance reminded it that "the late fury of the political heavens having spent itself in the fierce and bitter contests which raged in these halls, we have now a comparative quiet."[23] Then, because of his strong love for the Union, he expressed his desire for the well-being of the republic:

It may be the new tranquil skies do not portend—
            "A greater wreck, a deeper fall
            A shock to one, a thunderbolt to all."
But let us hope not. I, for one, am determined to interpret the omens for good. I hope . . . that the lull is not a treacherous stillness, heralding the deadly simoom, but that it is Halycon herself who comes to brood upon the dark and restless deep.[24]

Vance had observed hopeful signs in the first eight weeks of the session. In spite of the grave and serious questions that had been discussed, harmony and good feeling had prevailed. There had been two speeches that almost succeeded in reviving a sectional battle over slavery, but they fell a little short of their purpose.

Vance considered it the duty of Congress to take advantage of this hopeful state of affairs, and to give attention to the practical matters of the nation. "Too long," he said, "has the country suffered from this all-absorbing excitement which has so much hindered practical legislation." The practical legislation to which he referred was necessitated by disordered finances, depressed trade, an empty treasury, and a confused foreign policy.

Trying to remain neutral as far as sectional differences were concerned, Vance stated:

I am, ... like those I represent, opposed to a tariff for protection ..., because it is to the interest of my section. I place it upon the ground of self interest frankly, because I do not believe in the validity of the general rules and deductions, which gentlemen lay down so fluently. To assert that the only true policy of a nation is free trade is only less absurd than to assert that the nation should extend protection, universally, to all the manufactures within its borders. Trade and manufacturing are, I take it, governed and affected like all other human transactions by the thousand and one accidents and adventitious circumstances to which nations as well as individuals are subjected. What Adam Smith, and later British politicians, may say, in general terms, would have little more application to our condition, than would the maps and profiles of Professor Bache's survey applied to the angles and indentations of the British coast.[25]

Vance, thus far in his speech, had been realistic and only slightly partisan. His were the views of a moderate Whig, but even those were opposed by most Southern Democrats. His predecessor in Congress, Thomas Clingman, who was a native of Vance's section of North Carolina, addressed the Senate three days after Vance's speech, and denounced any increase in duties.[26]

In the second point of the speech Vance veered even farther from the southern view on public lands. Believing that public lands should not be a source of natural revenue, he denounced the Democrats. They had taken "ground against distribution and [had] declared that these lands ought to be held as a source of revenue.[27] Vance was confident that "every state in the union would have been materially enhanced, and the country saved from much wrangling and bitterness,"[28] if the proceeds of the land sales had been distributed to the states. These funds would have enabled the states to "erect public works, establish free schools, and to bear the burdens of general improvement within their respective borders."[29] Moreover, he showed the injustices and inequalities of the policy to states such as Virginia, North Carolina, and Georgia. These states had ceded their lands to the government, and all had been sold without any reduction in their tax load.

To keep his attack from appearing as a sectional one, Vance admitted that states in both the North and the South had shared in the spoils, but he arraigned the government for "swindling itself out of two-hundred million acres to build the Pacific railroad."[30]

Vance's objection was of a different nature. It was as a distributionist rather than as a Southerner that he declared:

If this fund is no longer to go into the public treasury to relieve the people from the burdens of a high tariff, why then, in common justice and common honesty, let us all, the old and the new states, take, share and share alike. I have long been a distributionist, because I thought justice and equality demanded it; but if I could only see these promises faithfully carried out, if I can only see this vast fund honestly applied to defraying the general charge and expenditure of a common government, I would agree to ask nothing more. I call on gentlemen to stop this wild raid after public lands. I will gladly stand with any party to affect this object.[31]

In the final section of his speech, Vance exhibited humanitarian impulses as he spoke in behalf of the old soldiers of the War of 1812. The Old Soldiers Pension Bill, granting pensions to the veterans of this war, was threatened by an economy wave. To Vance, this was an attempt to economize in the wrong place.

I do not wish ... to let the first stroke fall on the best, the noblest, the most useful part of the whole nation, the gallant soldiers of the War of 1812. What would be the thought ... of the man who would begin to reform his household expenses, by giving a half feed to his horse, his ox, and his plowman? Instead of saving money, ... he would dry up the source entirely; for in a short time, his plowman and his horse would be as weak as a politician's promise, as feeble as a modern platform. Such a man ... would be called a fool, and would deserve the appellation. He should commence by cutting off all the superfluous parts of his establishment first, so there might be no diminution in the comforts of those who labored. So ... we should begin in the national household, to lop off the superfluous excrescences that uselessly feed on the treasury.[32]

The lesson in economy clearly stated, Vance strengthened his persuasive effort by a touch of pathos. "As [the soldiers] were prompt and brave to defend us," he said, "so should we be prompt and liberal to repay them." Honor and glory were not sufficient rewards. "Thousands of these men," he explained, "are now in the deepest poverty, and have the hardest work to keep the wolf from the doors of their homes, where dwell their wives and little ones. Can one of them walk into the market and buy a rump of beef or a leg of mutton with glory?"[33] Driving home the point that a man cannot live on glory, he told this story:

That argument ... reminds me of the customs in Catholic countries, of having the priest to pass over the fields in the spring and bless the expected crop. On one such occasion, the priest, being something of an agriculturist, paused at one field which was very poor and sterile; "Here, my friends," said he, "blessings will do no good; this field must have manure." The old soldiers ... value the glory they have acquired, no doubt; but they must have something that will do more good than empty fame.[34]

In this speech Vance exemplified a loyalty to the nation such as few Southerners were willing to condone during this period.

Steering clear of a sectional or partisan bias, he was as a soothing balm cast onto the turbulent waters of controversy. He did not deny that he sought the welfare of his own state; however, bitter fanaticism was not his method of reaching this goal. When Congress adjourned on March 3, 1859, Vance was ready to return to his native Buncombe, and to enter the political arena to seek a full term in Congress.

At this time a new political organization was in the making in North Carolina. Being no longer acceptable to many voters in the state,[35] the Know-Nothing party was abandoned and the old Whig party was revitalized with the safety of the Union as its slogan.[36]

In this political picture, Vance found himself the Whig candidate for re-election in the eighth district. Vance was happy to call himself a Whig, for he had never been able to subscribe to Know-Nothing principles. In his campaign speeches of 1858, he had made fun of its doctrines, and had become a member only because there was no other party he could join. Being a Unionist, he could not affiliate with the Democrats who believed too strictly in the doctrine of state rights.[37] Vance's aim was to break the hold of the Democrats on the people.

As the candidates opened the campaign, his opponent, Coleman, spoke first at a joint political rally in Asheville. His able speech made Vance's friends fear he could not satisfactorily answer it. The principal charge against Vance was that he had voted in Congress to pension the soldiers of the War of 1812. Answering this charge, Vance described the old veterans as rallying to the defense of the nation in order to secure "the peace that followed, and the easy times now in the country." Sarcastically, he explained that times were so good that certain leaders felt authorized to advocate an act to use millions of dollars in corrupting Spanish officials in an effort to secure Cuba.[38] This remark referred to President Buchanan, Pierre Soule, and John Y. Mason, who had drawn up the Ostend Manifesto, proposing that the United States offer a large sum of money to Spain for Cuba, and if Spain refused to sell, the United States would resort to drastic means to obtain it. Resorting to pathetic appeal, Vance pictured the old soldier on crutches asking Congress for a mere pittance of eight dollars a month "to smooth his passage to the grave." But that instead of receiving the money, the soldier was met at the door of the House of Representatives and told to go away because there were other uses for the money.

Towards the end of the campaign, Coleman applied to Vance the parable of the barren fig tree. He said that though Vance had been in Congress, there was no fruit to show for it. At this point Coleman cried out, "Fellow citizens, cut him down." When Coleman finished, Vance, who was skilled at turning the charges of an opponent to his own advantage, replied that Coleman's use of the Scriptures was unfortunate. The real facts were that when the Lord was in the garden with the gardener, and seeing no fruit on the fig tree, told the gardener to cut it down. The gardener answered, "Let it stand another year, and I will dig about it, and then if it bears no fruit, cut it down." "Now gentlemen," Vance said, "all things according to the scripture." He applied the parable to himself, saying that if he did not bear fruit after his opponent had dug about him, then "cut me down." That his answer was effective, was evidenced by the shouts of approval that went up from the audience.[39]

Soon the candidates were resorting to tactics of personal abuse.[40] Coleman, for example, indicted Vance for having spread a report that he was intoxicated when they spent a night together in Caldwell County.[41] When Vance did not offer a satisfactory defense to this charge, Coleman challenged him to a duel.[42] Vance accepted, and accused Coleman of desiring a quarrel in order to take away the sting of defeat. The duel was eventually averted by the intervention of friends, who persuaded Vance to write a letter of explanation and apology.[43]

Vance's impulsive nature in debate was a weakness of his campaign speaking. When the charges of his opponents became strong, he often became excited, and responded without judgment or tact.[44] As early as 1855, he was challenged to a duel for having called a political opponent a "damned liar" before a large crowd.[45] Coleman wrote that Vance's "language and bearing on various occasions during the discussions in [the 1859] canvass [were] such as a gentleman should not submit to from another gentleman."[46] Vance, believing that in political discussion he had license to say whatever he chose, was unable to understand why anyone should take offense at his remarks.[47]

Nevertheless, Vance's skill in reply, and his ability to pass at will from humor to invective, pleased his audiences as much as it offended his opponents.[48] He defeated Coleman by seventeen hundred votes.[49]

Vance began the first session of the thirty-sixth Congress as a peacemaker. Congress needed the cheerful, fun-making qualities that Vance brought to it since it was in a session of heated discussion on the slavery question, prompted by John Brown's raid, Hepler's *Impending Crisis,* and other abolitionist activities. Vance did not adopt a southern view, and southern rights men such as Jefferson Davis or Alexander Stephens received no support from him. Vance insisted that no problems before Congress should permit the nation to be led to war.[50]

The opening of Congress on December 9, 1859, brought a contest over the House speakership. The Republicans wanted John Sherman for speaker, while the Democrats, in caucus, had nominated Thomas S. Bocock. This meant that the party which could ally itself with the Know-Nothings and the Whigs would succeed.[51] Vance remained silent, but not indifferent, during the sectional battles that raged through the first weeks of the session. However, his silence ended, when his name was called on the twenty-fourth ballot in the speakership deadlock. He said, "I hope the House will indulge me in a single remark, especially in consideration of the fact that I have not trespassed upon its attention from the commencement of the present session until today." Then he explained:

I have voted for a Lecompton Democrat. I have voted for those who did not approve of the Lecompton bill. I have voted for an anti-administration Democrat. And if there is any member of that great prolific Democratic family that I have neglected, I hope they will trot him out and give me an opportunity to vote for him.[52]

Throughout the controversy, Vance demonstrated his loyalty to the Union. With a bit of irony to add the characteristic light touch to his speech, he explained his votes:

I hope I have shown by the votes that I have recorded here in this contest, that I am willing to assist in the election of any man upon a conservative and national basis — which phrase I am certain this House has never heard.[53]

As the laughter produced by this remark subsided, he ended his brief speech. The conclusion of the speech expressed his willingness to exhibit a national conservative spirit by voting for Charles L. Scott, a Democrat from California. By this speech, Vance lent his efforts to concentrate the House votes on one man.

The debate on the speakership continued into the new year. Speaking on January 3, 1860, Vance pleaded for the abolition of political prejudices for the common good. He arraigned the Southern Democrats for refusing to vote for John A. McClernand, a Democrat from Illinois.

Paving the way for his support of McClernand, Vance said that he did not believe in making a personal explanation for everything he had done, or of every vote that he might make. His constituents at home, not the members of the House, were the ones to whom he would have to answer for his conduct. He planned, however, to make a brief explanation in this case. Paraphrasing Shakespeare to serve his own thoughts, he introduced his explanation:

I profess to have a fee simple in my own understanding, though my understanding, like the fee may be simple also. But I propose, upon the occasion, very briefly — for brevity is the soul of wit; I should like, at least, to possess the sole wit of brevity — to make the vote I am now going to give, the occasion, rather than the subject, of a brief explanation.[54]

In voting for McClernand, Vance declared that he was only showing his opposition to Black Republicanism. Although he was a Whig, he did not want to see a breach between the Northern and and Southern wings of the Democratic party. He knew that such a breach would endanger the Union, and hence pleaded for tolerance:

I consider it an evidence of degeneracy of the times that gentlemen here can not sacrifice so small and insignificant a thing as their party prejudices for the common good, when men may be sometime called upon, as our fathers were in times past, to sacrifice their lives, their fortunes, and their heart's best blood to the cause of their country.[55]

In the presidential election of 1860, the Democrats were divided. The National Democratic party, representing the Northern faction, nominated Stephen A. Douglas. The Southern bolters formed the Constitutional Democratic party, and nominated John C. Breckinridge of Kentucky.

The Constitutional Union party was made up of Northerners as well as Southerners who distrusted both Douglas and Breckinridge. They were a peace-loving party made up chiefly of "old line Whigs," and the conservative older men of the South.[56] In spite of his youth, Vance became a standard bearer for the party's presidential candidate, John Bell of Tennessee, and emerged from the contest with a wider reputation as a stump speaker.

A great meeting of Whigs and Conservatives was held on October 11 and 12, 1860, at Salisbury, N. C. to protest the calling of a state convention to consider secession. Vance spoke for two hours during the afternoon of the first day of the meeting, and held the attention of a great crowd assembled in a cold drizzling rain. At every attempt to stop, he was greeted with shouts of "Go on, go on."[57] The sentiment expressed in the speech was that "we will fight for the constitution, the Union, and the laws, within the Union and the laws." He said, "We will not be influenced by seceders in the South or Black Republicans in the North, and we will never give up our institutions until stern necessity compels us to believe that they are no longer adequate to our protection; we must resort to that right of revolution, which is inherent in every people."[58] To put it simply, he rebuked both the secessionists of the South, and the abolitionists of the North, and in one great effort attempted to save the Union and the constitution.[59]

Approximately eight thousand people were gathered at Salisbury on the second day of the meeting. At night the crowd gathered in the public square to watch fireworks. From the beginning of the display, there were cries for "Vance," and "Let's hear the mountain boy." After an elaborate exhibition of fireworks, and more calls for him, Vance came forward and mounted a pile of boxes. After quieting his audience with a number of clever stories, he held their attention for over an hour. Cheer after cheer followed nearly every word he uttered. As he left the platform, the enthusiastic crowd threw wreaths over his head, and carried him on their shoulders through the audience with deafening shouts.[60]

In the campaign he continued his efforts to convince the people that they should work toward keeping North Carolina in the Union. He spoke in churches, as well as on the street corners, always saying, "Keep North Carolina in the Union! Let it not follow the example of the other Southern States."[61]

After the election of Lincoln, Vance continued as one of the foremost advocates of Unionism in North Carolina. In his position, he was supported by a majority of North Carolinians.[62] On November 30, 1860, two South Carolina members of Congress, William W. Boyce and John D. Ashmore, on their way to Washington to resign their seats, made disunion speeches to a large group in front of the Yarborough Hotel in Raleigh. It was known that the "mountain boy" was present, and soon the cry went up for "a speech from Vance." A bonfire was built in the street, and the courthouse was lighted. While Ashmore and Boyce were still speaking Vance was forced into the courthouse, but he refused to speak until his colleagues across the street had finished. Though it was after nine o'clock, the crowd filled the courthouse to hear him. The audience felt that he could furnish the antidote for the treasonous attempts made across the street "to alienate one portion of the country from another." His speech, which lasted for two hours, pleased all who wanted to preserve the Union.[63]

Introducing the speech with an anecdote, he told of the merchant's clerk who owned a beautiful spotted cat. A young lady customer wanted him to name the cat Julia, after her. With shyness he would not consent. Pressed to know why he would not give it the young lady's name, he blushed, and said it was not the "right sort of a cat." If anyone wanted to call this a disunion meeting, the name wouldn't fit any more than Julia would fit the cat.[64]

Vance then proceeded to show the folly of disunion. Ashmore and Boyce had argued that if the South should secede, it would have the blessings and protection of England. To this Vance replied that it would be a protection that "our forefathers had waged a seven years war to escape." His humble grandfather, Vance said, had shed his blood at King's Mountain to escape this protection, and now his grandson was called upon to fight to regain it. Arguing that England could not be depended upon to aid the South, he referred to an article in the London *Times* in which the Prince of Wales' visit to the slave pens at Richmond was treated as a blot upon the English character. He did not believe that slave property would be more secure under British protection than it was under the Constitution. To support this belief, Vance asked how many runaway slaves had been sent back by the British authorities in Canada?

In fairness to his South Carolina opponents, Vance was willing to agree to the correctness of some of their statements. He conceded that the legislation of most free states was disorganized and unfriendly, which in turn aided the escape of slaves from the border states. He also agreed that John Brown's raid was intolerable, and that a sectional president had been elected. Nevertheless, he was reassured by Lincoln's promise to be a national president, and felt that South Carolina had no grounds for taking the lead in the secession movement since she had suffered none from the election. On the other hand, Vance declared his willingness to go to the aid of Maryland, Kentucky, Virginia, and Missouri whenever they declared in respectful terms that the acts of the national administration were no longer tolerable. He then would be willing to join them in arms, dissolve the Union, and "let the Devil take the hindmost."[65]

Six weeks after Lincoln was elected, the South Carolina Convention had adopted an ordinance of secession, and by February, 1861, the entire lower South was out of the Union. North Carolina, together with most of the border states, remained in the Union.[66]

The second session of the Thirty-sixth Congress convened on December 3, 1860. Vance was a sober and quiet member, his only comments being some insignificant remarks on the state of the Union.[67]

The inauguration of Lincoln on March 4, 1861, marked the end of the Thirty-sixth Congress. It also marked the end of Vance's career in the House of Representatives. His term was to run through the Thirty-seventh Congress, but he was unable to serve because his state had joined the Confederacy before that Congress assembled.[68]

CHAPTER III

RHETORIC OF A WAR GOVERNOR

Only the bombardment of Fort Sumter on April 12, 1861, followed by Lincoln's call for troops, could arouse North Carolina to action. When the news reached him, Vance was speaking before an armed group of angry citizens in his native county, Buncombe. With his hand extended, he was pleading for the preservation of the Union. In describing this speech, he said that his hand which was raised in gesture "fell slowly and sadly by a secessionist." With altered voice and manner, he then called upon his audience to volunteer "not to fight against but for South Carolina."[1]

Almost immediately after Fort Sumter, Vance was transformed from an ardent unionist to a secessionist fired with jealousy for the rights of his own state; he was especially resentful of Lincoln's policy of coercion. On May 20, 1861, North Carolina reluctantly declared its independence and joined the Confederate States.[2]

Vance immediately became more than a platform supporter of the Confederacy. He organized a company of mountain boys from his native county into the "Rough and Ready Guards." This company, with Vance as Captain, saw lively action in the early fighting in North Carolina and in the Seven Days' battle before Richmond.[3]

The people, already suffering economic dislocations, were disheartened by a series of defeats on the coast. Supplies were quickly exhausted, and blockade runners were unable to provide necessary imports in sufficient amount. The entire state now became discontented over the high prices charged for every commodity, and the politicians in control of the state administration were blamed for conditions. Since the summer of 1861, the old-line

24

Whigs had been using this political discontent to build up a new political organization, called the Conservative party. One of the principal leaders of this new party was W. W. Holden, who had been thrown out of the Democratic party in 1860, because of his opposition to secession. Holden was editor of the Raleigh *Standard,* and he used this medium to criticize the Confederate government.[4]

The Raleigh *Standard* announced that a meeting would be held on May 21, 1862, for the purpose of expressing a preference for governor.

To find a candidate who could defeat the Confederate opposition was a herculean task for the Conservatives. Except for intimate talks with his soldiers, Vance's voice had been silenced by the noise of battle; however, he was still a favorite of the people. He agreed to leave the army and run for governor, feeling that he was definitely the peoples' choice and that it was his duty to abide by their will. Fittingly, he became the candidate on the people's ticket as announced in the *Standard,*[5] thereby giving the citizens of the state an opportunity to reward him for his leadership in the Twenty-Sixth Regiment of North Carolina.

Adhering to the request of such newspapers as the Wilmington *Journal,* which urged that there be no public speaking in the campaign and that the people refuse to vote for any candidate who engaged in speaking, Vance made only a few speeches, and these were to the soldiers. The campaign was influenced more by writing and less by speaking than any in which Vance was ever involved. In fact, the campaigning was left almost entirely to the newspapers who vigorously attacked and praised both candidates. Those favoring William Johnston, the Confederate candidate, said that if Vance were the fine soldier that he was claimed to be, he should stay in the field. In refutation, Vance's supporters contended that if Johnston were the ardent Southerner he professed to be, he should be in the field.[6]

Vance's opponents feared the effects his election would have on the course of the War. The *Raleigh Register,* which had been an old-line Whig paper and at one time an admirer of Vance, carried this admonition: "Remember that if Zebulon Vance shall be elected governor, the Yankees will claim it is an indubitable sign that the Union sentiment is in the ascendancy in the heart of the Southern Confederacy."[7] The most disturbing factor involved in the campaign, however, was Vance's alliance with Holden. The *Register* warned that the election of Vance would amount to the election of Holden.[8] Holden's paper, the *Standard,* had given the impression of unfriendliness to the Southern cause,[9] and the Confederates sincerely feared that Vance might follow the same course.

Despite the efforts of the Confederate party to defame Vance with such epithets as "Yankee candidate" and "pliant tool of Holden," public confidence in his ability and loyalty elected him to the governorship in August, 1862, by a vote of 54,423 to 20,448 for Johnston.[10] The election took place while his regiment was encamped at Petersburg, Virginia, and Vance received every vote cast by the regiment.[11]

Before he left the army, two thousand soldiers gathered out-of-doors at night to offer tribute to their departing commander. L. L. Polk, sergeant major of the regiment, presented a sword to Vance on behalf of the officers. In response, Vance made a speech which was described as one the soldiers could not easily forget.[12]

On Saturday afternoon, August 16, the governor-elect arrived in Raleigh. That evening a group of admirers and interested people gathered in front of the Yarborough House where he was staying, and called for a speech. Although he was weary from travel and weakened in health from the rigors of battle, he made a twenty-nine minute speech which satisfied the Conservatives and pleased the Confederates.[13] He promised "unremitting prosecution of the war, and pledged himself to eschew all action founded on mere partisan considerations." Except for a bit of satire, this speech differed from those typical of Vance in that it was serious from beginning to end. Indeed, when one of his admirers asked for a joke, he replied that the time for joking had for the present "dried up."[14]

Opening the speech with a personal introduction, Vance sought to gain the favorable attention of his audience. He expressed thanks for the compliment that was implied in their election of him, and declared that the people had by this act taken their affairs into their own hands. A portion of his introduction was designed for those in his audience who might regard him with partisan hostility or suspicion. To eliminate such attitudes, he said, "In spite of feeble attempts to create and array parties in the midst of war, the people had declared by their vote that they would have none of it."[15]

During the campaign, he continued, his opponents had made many unjust attacks upon him. Perhaps he was too sensitive to those who suggested that he had not actually participated in the fighting at the time he had been engaged in the severe battles at New Bern and Malvern Hill. Resorting to one of his characteristic forms of attack, he used satire to reduce his opponent's assertions to absurdity, declaring he had been of the opinion that he was in those fights. To illustrate this fact satirically, he related the following story showing that he was of the same frame of mind as one of the clients of a lawyer named McDuffie:

That great advocate made a speech in defense of his client which drew tears from the court, the jury, the audience, the women, children and all, and the result was he was acquitted. After he had paid Mr. Mc-Duffie his fee, which was a good one, of course, the latter said to him, calling him by name — "You are certainly guilty of that crime." "Not a bit of it," responded his client. "I thought I was guilty before you made that speech, but I am certain now that I am not." I thought I was in both those fights; but after the efforts made to prove that I was not, I am willing to admit that I was not there — though I do retain an indistinct recollection of the bullets that whistled around my ears.[16]

The approval of his audience was clinched when he closed the attack by stating that " there was one thing . . . which he felt sure his opponents would admit, and that was that he was in the race for governor."[17]

With the completion of his introduction, Vance had, indeed, in the words of Cicero, "render[ed] the audience well disposed, attentive, and open to conviction." He then stated his proposition for discussion, in an effort to convince his audience that the great absorbing purpose of the state should be "to beat back our invaders and establish the independence of this glorious Confederation of States." The fact that he had been accused of wanting to take North Carolina back into the Union was monstrous, he said, and as proof he offered the following rhetorical questions in parallel style:

Was it for this that North Carolina solemnly dissolved her connection with that government? Was it for this that she had organized nearly sixty regiments, and had poured out her treasure and the blood of her sons like water, on every battle-field, from that of great Bethel to the crowning victories below Richmond? Was it for this that our people were submitting cheerfully to all kinds of privations at home, while our brave boys were daring disease, and wounds, and captivity, and death in the face of the enemy? Was it for this that our women and children had contributed of their household goods — the work of their delicate fingers — uncounted stores of provisions for our troops, encouraging those who were already in the field, and bidding others to go to their aid? Was it for this that many of these women and children, on hundreds and hundreds of farms, were toiling day by day in the burning sun with bare feet, following the plough, handling the hoe and axe, that they might produce and gather harvests for sustenance while their husbands and fathers and sons and brothers were engaged in the fight?[18]

The speech was concluded with a tribute to the soldiers of North Carolina and with praise for the state. He ended the address in the midst of enthusiastic applause.[19]

In less than a month Vance again faced an audience. Four or five thousand people gathered in Raleigh on September 8, 1862, to see him inaugurated.

Although Vance was only thirty-two years of age, he was fully aware of the enormous responsibilities the governorship placed upon him. Referring in his exordium to the oath of office he had just taken, he declared, "I can but feel oppressed by the great weight of responsibility." With a feeling of humility at the confidence of the people in calling him "with a unanimity unparallelled in the history of [the] state," he reviewed the task that was his. As he saw it, his duties were "to hold the helm during ... the great storm; to manage ... public liabilities; to search out the talent and worth of the country and to bring it into the service of the State; and to clothe and organize our troops and to do justice to merit on the field."[20] Such an undertaking was, he declared, enough to astound statesmen far older than himself, but he was ready and willing to accept the responsibility.[21] With strong ethical appeal, he ended his introduction with a solemn promise "to bring a will and determination to the performance of my duties which no one can surpass."[22]

If before his inaugural address there had been doubt as to where Vance stood regarding the conduct of the war, there certainly was none at the conclusion. Vance centered his remarks in "one great all-absorbing theme" — a plea for North Carolina to be faithful in the performance of her part in the great struggle, so that the Confederate states could stand proudly among free and independent nations.[23]

In defending North Carolina's entry into the war, Vance declared there was no alternate road the state could have pursued. Explaining that North Carolina had adopted a wait-and-see policy after the election of Lincoln, Vance blamed him for forcing the state into war. In fact, Vance absolved North Carolina of any responsibility, and fully justified its action. In support of this position, he declared that while North Carolina was engaged in an effort to persuade the North to allow people to resist secession by discussion or violence, Lincoln issued a proclamation calling for seventy-five thousand men to slaughter the Southern states into submission. The federal government then demanded that North Carolina provide a proportionate share of these troops "to step across the state line, and hand in hand with the scum of northern cities and the refuse of degradation . . . cut the throats of our kindred and friends."[24]

Although Vance had not belonged to that group of Southerners known as the rabid fire-eaters, he believed strongly in their concept of state rights. While he wanted to remain in the Union, he believed it to be a confederation of independent states held together by a written compact.

At the time of the inauguration, the war had been raging for seventeen months. Vance was, of course, familiar with the progress that the Confederate army had made during these months, because he had been in the midst of the fighting. He used a portion of the address to picture vividly the progress of the war in phrases abounding in pathos:

For seventeen months has this unequal war progressed; the many against the few; the powerful against the weak; and yet army after army, as the sands of the sea in numbers, led by vaunted Napoleons, and armed from the workshops of Europe have been hurled back from our capital with slaughter and disgrace, by troops in many cases, ragged, barefooted and armed with the condemned muskets of the old government![25]

Vance attributed the success of the Confederate army to the special favor of God. Illustrating by Biblical allusion, he declared, "The bush has indeed burned with fire, but is not consumed because of the presence of the living God."

There were some in the audience who were suspicious of Vance's views about the war. He had been aligned too closely with Holden for them not to be concerned. They feared that he would turn his back on the Southern cause, and try to lead North Carolina back into the Union. These doubts were soon dispelled, however, and his loyalty to the state and the Confederacy were sustained with a positive rebuke of those "who for the sake of peace would leave their children a heritage of shame." "Is there yet a man," he asked, "in the gallant historic state of North Carolina,

so embedded in political dogmas as to be unmindful of the claims
of his country, not to hear the great blows which are shaking the
continent for him and his children?"

The Conscription Act which the Confederate Congress passed
in April, 1862, had become extremely unpopular in North Carolina. The soldiers thought it unethical and discriminatory; many
lawyers declared it unconstitutional; the people considered it un-
necessary, undemocratic, and unjust.[26] Recognizing his audience's
antagonistic attitude toward the act, Vance pleaded for obedience
to it:

Many of you thought it [the Conscription Act] harsh and unconstitutional; it *was* harsh, and *may* have been unconstitutional, though many
of our ablest statesmen thought not. To stop now to argue it could
only produce the greatest mischief, for the reason that it has already
been executed upon at least four fifths of those subject to it. However,
objectional in its conception, let us, at least, be just and impartial in
its execution. But I am sure that if every man who has his country's
good at heart but knew of the necessity which existed at the time, he
would render it cheerful obedience. Within five weeks of its passage,
one hundred and forty seven of our best trained and victorious regiments would have been disbanded. And this during the very darkest
days in the history of the war.[27]

Instead of asking his audience to accept a generalized statement,
he showed a familiarity with the requirements of sound argument
by supplying evidence to prove that the act was passed during the
darkest days in the history of the war. Many adversities had confronted the South, and these Vance used to support his position.
Fort Donelson and Nashville had fallen to the enemy, and General Halleck, with a large iron-clad fleet, had passed into the heart
of the South. McClellan's well-equipped army "was in the act of
springing, as a tiger, upon Richmond" as soon as he was assured
of success by the disbanding of the South's troops. Within North
Carolina, Roanoke Island and New Bern, with their dependencies
upon the coast, were possessed by the enemy, as were much of
South Carolina and Georgia.

The Conscription law was passed and the country was saved, but only, he declared, through the patriotic endurance of the soldiers in the field.

> . . . they swallowed down their bitter sorrow, they dismissed all hopes of seeing their homes and families, grasped their muskets and set again their resolute faces toward the flashing of the guns. God bless them for it! An exhibition of purer patriotism has not been seen on the continent, and our government can never sufficiently appreciate it.
>
> I remember with a thrill of pride, the conduct of the gallant men I so lately was honored by commanding. They too were discontented and spoke loudly and bitterly against the harshness of the law. I called them together and simply laid before them the necessities of their country and appealed to their patriotism to sustain it; I made them no promises, held out no hopes; I even told them that though they were promised furloughs by the law, they would not get them; that there was nothing before them but fighting and suffering. They quietly dispersed to their quarters, and in four hours the regiment was re-organized for war! . . .
>
> If they who went out first, and have suffered and bled from the beginning, could thus submit, Ah! Can not those who have so far reposed in peace in their protected homes give the remainder of their time to their country. Our brave regiments have had their ranks thinned by death and disease; will you not all go cheerfully to their help? They have struggled for you and now you are needed to struggle with them.[28]

There were, moreover, duties to be performed at home as well as on the battlefield. Vance was aware of what they were, and declared, "Let those of us who remain at home bend every energy to the task of clothing and feeding our defenders in the field and providing for their wives and children." He held that the first concern of the state should be for the care of the families of its soldiers, and to this end he asked for an "imitation of that heroic self-denial by which our mothers of the first revolution rendered their names worthy of a bright place in history. . . ."[29]

The peroration of the address possessed a dignity and eloquence typical of the formal speaking of the era. Humor was replaced by vivid figures of speech designed to gain interest. The mood was serious, because there were urgent problems to be solved. Optimistic prophecy, however, overshadowed any gloom as the speaker proclaimed in metaphorical language that "the womb of the future, I am confident, holds for us a bright and glorious destiny."[30] He proclaimed that "the vast armies which invaded us at the beginning of the year have melted away like frost before the steady valor of our troops. . . . "[31]

As he closed his address in what one would term the grand style, he reinforced in eloquent language a true devotion to the struggle in which North Carolina was engaged. With a strong forthright plea for sacrificial action from the people, he ended the speech by saying:

Oh, my Countrymen, let us resolve this day that . . . North Carolina, at least, shall not fail in the performance of her part, that the streams of precious blood with which our glorious sons have consecrated their names to immortality, shall not be a vain and unaccepted sacrifice, but through the valor and determination of those who survive they shall be rendered efficacious to the salvation of the Nation; and with hearts strong for the mighty task, and purpose united, we will give of our substance — give of our blood; we will toil and struggle, we will suffer and endure, through all the dreary watches of the night until the day star of independence, flashing through the darkness in the east, shall fill the whole earth with his beams.[32]

Vance did not resort again to the public platform until the spring of 1865. His work was laid out for him when he took office, and action had to take precedence over talk during these perilous days. There was insufficient food and clothing for the soldiers, and their wives and children were completely destitute. Consequently, the governor tried immediately to relieve the suffering which the war had brought. Instead of making speeches, he, from time to time, wrote addresses to the citizens of the state and published them in the newspapers.

Vance's first message to the legislature followed the pattern of the addresses he had been writing to the people since his inauguration. He showed his chief concern to be that of supplying food and clothing for the citizens and soldiers of the state. The message, which was patriotic, wise, and practical, recommended that steps be taken to prevent exportation, except to the army or to a sister state, of such provisions as cotton, cloth, salt, leather, and other essentials. This recommendation was designed to eliminate speculation by unscrupulous persons. In order to relieve the suffering of the wives and children of the soldiers, he urged that corn and pork be purchased and stored, and that it then be sold to citizens at rates just sufficient to cover the cost of transportation. To prevent Tarheel soldiers from having to fight in their bare feet as they had done at Boonsboro and Sharpsburg, he recommended that the legislature place an embargo upon leather. He believed this action would prevent the Confederate government and the speculators from competing for leather.[33]

Early in his administration, Vance also turned his attention to the problem of driving federal troops from North Carolina soil. He began a correspondence with the Confederate authorities in Richmond, demanding that reinforcements be sent to protect the eastern counties.[34] This attitude made few friends among members of the Confederate administration for Vance, but it enhanced his popularity with his fellow Tarheels.

Although he was out of the line of battle, Vance was cognizant of and interested in the needs of the soldiers in the field. Soon after his inauguration, he visited the Fifty-Sixth Regiment which had camped at Cross Roads Church near Tarboro. Here he talked to the men and led them to look upon any sacrifice that might be offered in the name of "the good old North State," as a privilege.[35]

Vance's sanction of the war eventually led to a rift between him and W. W. Holden, who had been his strongest supporter for the governorship. By the spring of 1863, people began to talk of peace and reconstruction, and Holden's role in this movement was responsible for the breach between the two friends.

Holden believed that Vance would join in the peace movement as a means of securing better treatment for North Carolina from the Confederate government. He had miscalculated the governor's nature, however, and soon learned that Vance could be controlled by no one. Although they both were "peace men," they were far apart in their views as to how peace should be obtained. Vance was willing to make peace in cooperation with the other Confederate states, while Holden proposed that North Carolina should make a separate peace with the national government if necessary.

Vance remained relatively silent — at least in public — on the peace movement until September 10, 1863, when he issued a proclamation condemning public meetings in which threats of resistance to the laws of the Confederate government had been made. At the same time he protected the rights of the peace men as willingly as he did the laws of the Confederacy. A few days after his proclamation attacking the peace meetings, a Georgia brigade under General Henry T. Benning stopped in Raleigh while passing through to Tennessee. Members of the brigade became embroiled with a number of Holden's friends, and one of the regiments went to the office of the *Standard* and almost demolished it. As soon as the governor received the alarm from a guard, he rushed to the scene and demanded that the destruction stop. He spoke to the rioters in eloquent but angry tones, telling them that he regretted seeing such brave men engaged in so disreputable a work, and was pained to know that "a blow had been struck at the dearest rights of a private citizen — rights purchased by the richest blood of their patriotic fathers in defense of which every man among them should be ready to lay down his life." Vance vowed to defend Holden as well as every citizen of the state. After he concluded his speech, an officer assured him that there would be no further violence, and in the midst of cheers for Vance the soldiers marched off to camp. Early the next morning, another mob gathered in the market and proceeded to demolish the office of the *State Journal*. If Vance had not arrived on the scene to speak to them, they would have destroyed the *Raleigh Register* as well. After listening to Vance the lawless crowd, pledged to Holden, cheered both Vance and Holden as they disbanded.[36]

Although opposed to Holden and the peace movement, Vance could not bring himself to denounce openly a man who had been so instrumental in his election. He was disturbed by Holden's peace efforts, as well as by other evidences of discontent in North Carolina, and in a desperate move wrote to President Davis. He suggested to Davis that negotiation with the enemy was the only possible way in which to remove the discontent.[37] To this Davis replied that the Confederate administration had made "three distinct efforts to communicate with authorities at Washington and have been invariably unsuccessful." Therefore, there was nothing more that could be done by the administration in Richmond, but he thought there was much that Vance could do. "With your influence and position," he said, "the promoters of the unfounded discontents now prevalent in your state, would be put down without the use of physical force, if you would abandon a policy of conciliation, and set them at defiance."[38]

Early in 1864 Vance realized that the final plunge, which would separate him from many of his political friends, had to be made. Holden and his cohorts were planning a convention in May to take North Carolina back into the Union. Vance strongly opposed this action, and vehemently declared that he could never consent to this course. Believing "that it would bring ruin alike to state and Confederacy," he vowed, if the peace movement should be inevitable, "to quietly retire to the army and find death which will enable my children to say that their father was not consenting to their degradation." Vance thought that the withdrawal from the Confederacy would "steep the name of North Carolina in infamy,"[39] and declared that he would "see this Conservative party blown into a thousand atoms and Holden and his understrappers in hell" before he would consent to such a course.[40]

In opposing Holden's peace movement, Vance had decided to become a candidate for re-election as governor. He believed he could best accomplish this by taking the stump early and devoting all his time and strength in "trying to warn and harmonize the people."[41] Consequently, he began preparations for an unprecedented speaking tour, which resulted in a memorable campaign with Holden as the opposition candidate.[42]

CHAPTER IV

THE CAMPAIGN OF 1864

Amid the furor of petitions and resolutions, Vance was also confronted with army desertions and other forms of disaffection. Since the summer of 1863, the central government at Richmond had been concerned about disaffection in North Carolina, but not until February, 1864, did it take any positive action. Reports had reached Vance early in February that Congress and President Davis were resolved upon passing a bill suspending the writ of habeas corpus throughout the Confederacy. Believing that the bill was directed specifically against North Carolina, Governor Vance wrote to Davis advising him "to be chary of exercising the powers" with which it would invest him.[1]

Plans were already under way for him to begin his stump-speaking campaign at Wilkesboro on February 22, when he wrote to Davis. He had been assured that thousands would be present if the weather were good. The consensus of his Wilkesboro friends was that the deserters would come out to hear him if they were granted amnesty, and many of them would be persuaded by Vance to return to the army.[2] This assurance from Wilkesboro may have encouraged Vance's faith in his ability to restrain the revolutionary tendency of public opinion which he expressed in a letter to Davis.[3]

He kept his appointment to speak at a Washington's birthday celebration in Wilkesboro, a mountain town in the heart of the state's most disaffected territory. Here he began his campaign for re-election by publicly repudiating W. W. Holden. This speech of immense length was delivered before an audience of about two thousand people. In his introduction Vance referred to the size of his audience by relating a humorous anecdote:

I do not know how it is possible for me to make myself heard by this large audience, unless I adopt the plan of the one armed soldier who could not hug his sweetheart all the way around, and so was forced to chalk the distance he could reach on one side and then turn and hug as far on the other.[4]

The Wilkesboro speech is probably as good an example of audience adaptation as can be found anywhere in his speeches. Vance was mild and conciliatory, especially in his discussion of the suspension of the writ of habeas corpus. "I went to ease those fellows off," he said in a later speech as he was explaining why he did not vigorously condemn the suspension of the writ in his Wilkesboro speech.[5] He both praised and blamed the administration at Richmond, but he was careful not to antagonize his audience.

Before setting forth the theme of his message, Vance made sure that his character as a speaker was firmly established. Perhaps he recalled the place of ethical appeal which he had learned from his rhetoric classes at the university when he said:

I shall endeavor to justify both the public interest you display and the compliment you bestow, by today doing something which is very rare in a politician — by telling the truth . . . you desire to hear about the condition of the country. Of course you want the plain unadulterated facts, not that which would be most pleasing to you, but that which was true. You would be unable to find a demagogue who would comply with this requirement, because with him the habit of telling the people that which flatters their vanity and carefully avoiding any painful truth which might shock their tender sensibilities has grown into a second nature from which we may anticipate no substantial food for the body politic such as these trying times imperatively demand. . . . I am not so hypocritical as to boast that in all my past career I have never once talked "soft nonsense" to the "dear people." On the contrary, I am free to confess that otherwise I would not have been a successful suitor for political favors. But I flatter myself, I have preserved enough honor and candor to prevent me, when so urgent a necessity requires it, from telling that which is most pleasant in preference to that which is most true, and from trifling with the destinies of my country. I esteem myself very fortunate in having saved so much as this from the breakers whereon so many craft go to pieces in the yeasty waves of political life. Indeed I may say I am as lucky as Paddy Maquire, an old acquaintance of my friend ... who, in reply to the friendly inquiry of the latter, how he got on, exclaimed, "Well may it please yer honor, I've bin upon yer state docket an' bin drunk, an' got a flogging at the whippin' post since ye was here; but thanks be to the Vargin amid all me wickedness and raskhality, I've preserved me religion entire." And so amid all my political shortcomings I have preserved honesty enough, I hope, to tell you what I conceive to be true about the condition of the country) ... "[6]

Having established his *ethos*, Vance proceeded to present his central theme which was a portrayal of the condition of the country relative to its civil and military affairs, the prospects for the future, and the duties of the people in accomplishing the work to be done. Throughout the speech, as throughout the entire campaign, he relied upon humor to hold the attention and interest of the audience. Jokes and anecdotes were used to poke fun at the central government and at the same time place his audience in a good mood. He declared, for instance, that even the capture of Vicksburg had its bright side. With the Trans-Mississippi separated from the East, he facetiously remarked that "the people over there are lucky, for the supply of bad generals has been cut off, and they flourish a little better on that account than we do."[7]

Vance's humor in the Wilkesboro speech might be considered as lacking in propriety, but so rash a judgment should not be made without first analyzing his audience. Wilkes County had many extreme Conservatives to whom Holden appealed. Vance was convinced that he could not win the election without the support of these old Union men, and he believed that the best way for him to save his country was to preserve his influence with them.[8] Clearly he could not hope to win their confidence if he praised Davis, which he was not prone to do anyway. On the other hand, there were Democrats in the audience whom he did not want to antagonize by vehemently attacking the president. Therefore, he settled on a mild form of satire as a means of criticizing the Confederate government. This could not seriously offend the Democrats, and it would let the Conservatives know that Vance did not object to their abuse of Jeff Davis so long as they opposed the movement for a convention.

Although humor was used throughout the speech, it was never used without a purpose. It usually amplified or clarified a point the speaker wished to make, just as did the story of the old lady who often rode horseback to the country store with her husband. Major Smith, who operated the store, always took the couple to the cellar to give them a sampling of his wet goods in order that he might sell them more of his dry goods when they had come back upstairs. On one trip they both had too much to drink, and on the way home the old lady fell off into the creek. When her husband missed her, he rode back and found her lying flat on her back with the water dammed up to her mouth. Believing she was still in the Major's cellar, she lay there rolling her eyes and pursing her lips as she said, "Not any more, I thank you Major, not another drop unless it is sweetened." Vance claimed to be more determined about secession than the old lady was about drinking. He wanted not another drop of it — sweetened or unsweetened.

At another point, he used humorous dialect to ridicule President Lincoln and to show that it would be dangerous for North Carolina to secede:

But what would Uncle Abraham say to it [secession] — that old gentleman whose personal pulchritude has been the subject of so much remark? And who they say can tell more jokes than I can — ... He would put his thumb up to his nose and make certain gyrations and evolutions with his finger and say: "Waul ole North Carolina, I'm tarnation glad ter see yer come outer Jeff Davis' little consarn, I swow; but yer don't mean to say yer ain't in the Union again, and the pertection of the best government the world ever saw. Bin fittin' yer too long to let you sneak out that way."[9]

The crude and earthy quality of his humor in no way detracted from its effectiveness, but rather appealed to the audience as well as strengthened the arguments. The speech was interrupted by laughter and applause wherever a humorous anecdote was used to support his views.[10] As long as Vance was able to keep the audience in a happy mood, he was sure that the people would listen to what he had to say.

The major portion of the speech was spent in condemning the peace movement and the calls for a convention. Vance, however, refrained from denouncing those who proposed a convention. Three reasons were given for his opposition to taking North Carolina out of the Confederacy and repudiating the rest of the South: (1) it would be useless to secede; (2) it would be dangerous; (3) it can't be done.

In support of the first argument, Vance utilized a hypothetical illustration to show that it would be as useless to secede from the Confederacy as it had been to secede from the Federal Union:

Now permit me to ask you what it was that got you into this scrape? Why, you all know it was the fact of your secession in the first instance. Suppose you were sick of typhoid fever and had been close to death's door; and becoming convalescent, the physician should gravely inform you that the only plan to effect your entire recovery would be to take another spell of the infernal fever. Would you not think he was a fool? Secession was tried after it had been considered for a period of forty years, and the whole country understood it as completely as an abstraction could be understood. We were promised it should be peaceable. What is the result, why, it has been everything else. It has involved us in a war that has no parallel upon the pages of history. Do you expect to find a remedy by a repetition of the dose that brought you to bed? Or suppose a surgeon would say to a soldier with a ball in his leg: "My dear fellow, I don't see how it is possible for you to obtain relief unless I call for another one and put another one in the other leg."[11]

If Vance appeared contradictory in professing the weakness of seceding from the Union, one has only to recall that he regretted leaving it, and "was one of the last to lay it down." Describing his feelings on leaving the Union he said that he did so "with the same mournful feelings with which I followed my dear father to the grave; I never expected and do not expect to see it resurrected."

A man should love his home if for nothing else but because it is his, and shelters him; he should love his wife if for no other reason than because she is his wife; he should love his state because it is his ... ; he should love his country right or wrong because in its destiny are involved the welfare of the state, community, home, wife, children, self. But if you have no other reason to give for defending it, say you do so because it is your country.[12]

Vance resorted to the use of both logic and emotion to convince the audience of the danger of pulling North Carolina out of the Confederacy. General Lee, he said, would send down his veterans to fall mercilessly upon a state which had abandoned the South. On the other hand, he argued that it would be preposterous to think that Lincoln would recognize the state's neutrality or abate his claims to allegiance and obedience. Instead, the state would be forced to enter the old Union and would have imposed on it a share of the debt, taxes, and burdens of the United States. "Instead of getting your sons back to the plow and fireside," he said, "they would be drafted and sent into the service of Uncle Sam, to fight along side of his Negro troops in extermination of the white men, women, and children of the South."

Supporting his final argument that North Carolina could not be severed entirely from the Confederacy, Vance generalized that the great mass of soldiers would not withdraw from battle and come home. With a series of emotionally packed phrases, he concluded that the soldiers who had "followed the old battle flag through smoke and fire, into the presence of death, and waved its bloody folds upon the height of an hundred fields of triumph" would not "trample it under foot and crawl upon their bellies and eat dirt in that sort of style."[13]

Having the ability to hold an audience's attention for almost any period of time, Vance was little concerned about the length of his speeches. In the Wilkesboro address, as was his common practice, he talked until he was confident that his persuasion had been achieved. After having presented his basic arguments against the withdrawal of North Carolina, he assured the audience that there were consequences other than those he had enumerated.

The first of the additional consequences was introduced by a rhetorical question. "What would become of the currency should you abandon the cause of the Southern Confederacy?" Noting that the condition of currency was already bad enough, he argued that since every bank in the state was filled with it, all of them would immediately be broken and worthless in the event of withdrawal from the Confederacy.

The second consequence was presented with all the pathos at the governor's command. None but the insensitive could have listened without compassion to his description of the plight that would befall the maimed and mutilated soldiers if the state should submit to the Union. With vivid imagery, he presented a dark picture for the crippled soldier:

> Having once submitted ourselves to the enemy, you might see one of them come up, his cheeks wan from suffering, his rags fluttering in the breeze, his wasted form supported on crutches, and ask the government for support. The reply would be: "You infamous rebel, have you the impudence to ask support from a government you have been fighting to destroy. No. You will get no pension; but we will tax as heavily as we can your little potato patch to pension the man who maimed you for life, desolated your home, insulted your mother." Could you endure such a spectacle?[14]

As a final consequence of submission Vance referred to President Lincoln's proclamation of December 8, 1863, which offered a plan of progressive reconstruction whereby the Union would be rebuilt as the war progressed. A pardon, with certain exceptions, was offered to any supporters of the rebellion who would take oath to support "the Constitution of the United States and the Union of the States thereunder" and "all acts of Congress passed during the existing rebellion, with reference to slaves. . . ." Lincoln promised further to recognize the government of any state in which a loyal nucleus equal to one-tenth of the votes cast in the presidential election of 1860 should take the oath and establish a state government with abolition of slavery.[15]

Typical of many of Vance's speeches, the peroration of the Wilkesboro address was obliquely suggestive, and was based upon a narrative from his favorite source, the Bible. As one may observe from the following passage, it was designed to motivate the audience to do nothing rash, and to maintain their goodwill to the very end:

In concluding, fellow-citizens, allow me to remind you of a text of Sacred Scripture which I think would suit your case. You know when St. Paul went to the City of Ephesus and announced the true God, he raised quite a row with Demetrius and the rest of the Artizans in the place, who had been accustomed to make their living by manufacturing shrines for the Goddess Diana and they were about to massacre St. Paul for his interference with their profits. At the height of the excitement which was about to break out into actual hostilities there appeared among them a fellow, the town clerk, who got upon the courthouse steps or stump and spoke to the people. He advised the people to do nothing rash. "For," said he, "you will be held accountable for this uproar."

I thank you for your indulgence with which you have attended my rambling remarks and in retiring allow me to express the hope and trust that ere many months, you may rest under the shade of our tree of national independence which has been so freely watered with blood and tears; within its leafy branches, the white winged dove of peace shall tune her soft note to the memory of your loved and lost, who rejoiced to lay down their lives for their altars and their firesides.[16]

The Wilkesboro speech stamped Vance with wide renown because it was the only one of the campaign that was stenographically reported. The *Richmond Enquirer* had a reporter present, and was the first paper to publish the speech in its entirety. Using this source, many North Carolina papers, and even the *New York Times,* reported the speech. Moreover, the speech was especially important because it set the pattern for the other speeches of the 1864 campaign, and in studying it one may become fully acquainted with the general theme and characteristics of his other campaign speeches.

Although Vance was confident of his success in the campaign, many of his supporters were fearful of the outcome. From many counties came reports of Holden's strength and the wavering loyalty of the people. Vance found himself in a precarious position in trying to determine the kind of campaign he should conduct. He felt obligated to abide by the requests from many of his friends for a wide speaking tour. On the other hand, the duties of his office required most of his time. He preferred to attend to his office duties, and to conduct the campaign in the same manner as he had conducted his first campaign. Finally, he realized that he must carry his campaign to the people. Everywhere he went he was warmly received. "This is the trouble with it," Vance said, "when I leave home once on a speaking tour I can with difficulty get back again. There is one thing very flattering in it, however, and which affords me much hope of success, and that is the immense crowds that turn out everywhere, even on the shortest notice."[17]

In response to urgent invitations from five or six brigades, Vance went to Virginia about the middle of March to visit the army. A grand review of the North Carolinians of the army was held during the first day. He delivered his first speech before a group of soldiers at Orange Court House, and his second at the headquarters of the Thirtieth North Carolina Regiment in the presence of General Lee and his veteran officers, as well as the soldiers.[18]

After being introduced for his second speech by General Ramseur, Vance sought to place his audience in a receptive frame of mind. This he did by resorting to the light touch. He said he had addressed them at the previous speech as "fellow soldiers," but on second-thought he recollected that although he once was a soldier, he was not one now that he had "skulked out of service by being elected to a little office down in North Carolina." He placed himself on common ground with them by telling them there was only one term that he could rightfully use and that was fellow-Tarheels.[19]

Throughout the speech he presented a ray of cheer and encouragement to the soldiers. He told them that prospects were never brighter, and with recruited and strengthened armies the people had become more cheerful. The fighting, he promised, would be virtually ended by the time the leaves began to fall in autumn if their troops could just hold their own. Continuing to proclaim the theme of his Wilkesboro speech, he declared there was only one way to gain peace, and that was by fighting for it. He considered it virtually impossible to negotiate peace with the enemy and he was violently opposed to any out-and-out separate state action. To persuade the soldiers to accept his view, he depicted the consequences of separate action and presented the degrading terms that Lincoln would demand of North Carolina.[20]

The speech accomplished its purpose in that it apparently cheered the soldiers, who received it enthusiastically. They were kept in broad grins throughout the address by Vance's inexhaustible supply of jokes.[21] General Lee declared that Vance's visit to the Army was equivalent to a reinforcement of fifty thousand men, and General Stuart remarked, "If the test of eloquence is its effect, this speech was the most eloquent ever delivered."[22]

After completing a series of patriotic addresses to the army, Vance returned to Raleigh where he found invitations to speak still converging upon him, some of them even suggesting that he and Holden appear on the same platform. Holden, however, refused to particpite in a joint debate on the ground that he did not want to add to the excitement of the time by "haranguing the people for their votes."[23] Vance, therefore, accepted the invitations to appear alone, and thus began an unprecedented speaking tour which covered the entire state. On April 22, 1864, he spoke in Fayetteville, where, in addition to proclaiming his own theme that there can be no peace by separate state action, he vigorously attacked Holden. Referring to his opponent, he said, "You all have heard of Holden. He wants my place. If he knew as much as I do about the place, he might not be anxious to get it." He confessed, however, that he was anxious to serve for another term since he had been removed from the army to serve the first term.

Vance also told the audience that he had invited Mr. Holden to come to Fayetteville, because he intended to speak of him personally and politically, and he preferred doing it face to face. Proceeding to read Holden's reply in which he had refused to come, Vance launched the following attack, with humor and sarcasm as the chief weapons:

He is so considerate that he don't [sic] want to take the people from farms. Mr. Holden says in his card he is not vain enough to hope to change any man's vote by speaking. Innuendo, Governor Vance is thus vain. . . . He does not wish to excite the people by haranguing them. Well, let him retire from the canvass and there will be no excitement. He says, "My principles are well known." Are they? Who knows them? One may know what principles he professed five years ago, and what opposite principles he professed six weeks ago. But who can tell what changes they have undergone in the last six weeks.[24]

While Vance carried his campaign directly to the people, Holden vigorously defended himself and made counter charges against Vance through the columns of his newspaper, the *Weekly Standard.*

Vance seemed to win the hearts of all the men, women, and children when he spoke, as was shown by the great numbers who came forward to shake his hand after each speech. He seemed to win the hearts of all the people. His popularity, however, cannot be attributed to his speaking alone because, as the Raleigh *Weekly Conservative* remarked:

He is the friend of the soldier, he clothes him; he is the friend of the widow, he sends her cotton cards, so desired by the thousand at the price of $5.00 in Confederate money; and he is in advance of Brown and Stephens for peace and the maintenance of law and order.[25]

Vance continued his strenuous speaking pace throughout the remainder of the campaign. From a schedule of his speaking engagements, it appears that he visited practically every city and hamlet in the state,[26] speaking somewhere every day and often at several places in a day.

In an effort to keep his speeches from becoming stale, Vance relied upon wit and caustic remarks to give them freshness. Although he gained much popularity from his use of wit and humor, he received much criticism from it also. After his Wilkesboro speech, scores of letters commending his efforts were written to him, but there were some which pronounced opposition to what was termed the "uttering of vain expressions."

On August 1, just three days before the election, Vance made one of the last speeches of the campaign to a large audience in the town theatre in Wilmington. After being greeted with warm applause, he spoke for two and one-half hours, using the arguments and style that were generally known because of his visits to every part of the state during the campaign. Asserting that he made no claims to perfection or infallibility, he was confident, he said, that he had done his best as governor, and he believed that his administration met the approval of the people of the state. He showed the inconsistencies of Mr. Holden's political course during which he had been a "Henry Clay, hard-cider drinking Whig; a Jackson, Union Democrat; a Calhoun, secession Democrat; and a Conservative of the straitest sect. In fact he was anything, everything, or nothing as he thought it might be popular."[27] With this final characterization of his opponent, Vance was ready for the people to decide in whose hands they wanted to commit the destiny of their state.

As the election day approached, the great issue before the people was: Shall North Carolina seek peace "on terms less than independence?" The people were ready to give the answer. Vance had won the support of the Confederates and the moderate Conservatives by his platform and his skill in oratory. The soldiers balloted in July before the rest of the citizenry, and they gave Vance 13,209 votes out of 15,033 votes. The defeat of Holden fully materialized on August 4 when the electorate gave Vance 57,873 votes to 14,432 votes for Holden, who carried only three counties — Randolph, Johnston and Wilkes.[28] Vance's victory clearly showed that the people opposed a separate peace and would continue to support the Confederacy even though they were not in full agreement with its government. Moreover, the vote completely refuted the belief that North Carolinians wanted peace at any cost.

CHAPTER V

DISCOURAGEMENT, DEFEAT, PRISON

The decisive defeat of Holden and the peace movement he fostered was a personal triumph for Vance. He was elated over his success and proudly boasted, "I have beaten him worse than any man was ever beaten in North Carolina."[1] Vance's high spirits however, were short lived as he observed the state of military affairs. Atlanta had already fallen into the hands of Sherman, who was planning to join Grant in Virginia. Lee's hold on Petersburg was precarious. If it should fall, the fall of Richmond would follow. It was in a mood of despair that Vance wrote to D. L. Swain:

I never before have been so gloomy about the condition of affairs. Early's defeat in the Valley I consider as the turning point in the campaign, and confidentially, I fear it seals the fate of Richmond though not immediately. It will require our utmost exertions to retain our footing in Virginia until 1865 comes in. McClellan's defeat is placed among the facts, and abolitionism is rampant for four years more. The army in Georgia is utterly demoralized, and by the time the president, who has gone there, displays again his obstinacy in defying public sentiment and his ignorance of men in the change to a still worse commander, its ruin will be complete. They are now deserting by hundreds. In short, if the enemy pushes his luck till the close of the year, we shall not be offered any terms at all. . . .[2]

Contributing to Vance's discouragement was his belief that the people were not behind the war effort. He was disturbed by the ease with which Sherman was able to march northward without opposition from North Carolinians. They had made no effort to destroy his lines of communication, and appeared to care little about the outcome of the war. Continuing his letter to Swain, Vance wrote:

49

The signs which discourage me more than all else is [sic] utter demoralization of the people. With a base line of communication 500 miles in Sherman's rear, through our own country not a bridge has been burnt, a car thrown from its tracks nor a man shot by a people whose country he has desolated. What does this show my dear sir? It shows what I have always believed, that the great popular heart is not now and never has been in the war! It was a revolution of the politicians not the people; was fought at first by the natural inclination of our young men, and has been kept going by state and sectional pride assisted by bitterness of feeling produced by the cruelties and butcheries of the enemy.[3]

The military defeats, and the demoralized spirit of the people were not the only causes for alarm. An economic depression had enveloped all of North Carolina. To ease the existing tensions, Vance called the Council of State together early in October and declared, with all the optimism at his command, that he expected the end of the war by the close of the year. Obviously, however, he was trying to build up courage. He pleaded with the Council to send more soldiers to Lee even if it meant placing state officers into service.[4]

The Council refused Vance's request to call a special session of the legislature, and decided to postpone dealing with the complex problems confronting the state until the regular session convened in the latter part of November. Vance delivered his message to the legislature on November 30, 1864, exactly two years after his first message. He expressed grave concern over the conditions within the state, and blamed the Confederacy for the state of affairs.

Relating the events which had taken place since the adjournment of the last legislature, Vance reported the fall of Plymouth and the evacuation of Little Washington. While these disasters were occurring in the eastern part of the state, he said that the western part of the state was being constantly raided by lawless men, many of whom were citizens of North Carolina. The majority of these men, who plundered, stole, and murdered, were deserters from the army which seriously needed them.[5] He admitted

that his proclamation promising pardon to all men who volun-
tarily returned to the army within thirty days had proved fruit-
less.[6] Unwilling to admit defeat, he declared that he could handle
the situation if the Confederate government would only release
the militia to him.[7]

A significant portion of the address was devoted to the resolutions which had been passed by a group of southern governors
meeting in Augusta, Georgia on November 17, 1864. The meeting, which had been instigated by Vance, was attended by the governors from Virginia, North Carolina, South Carolina, Georgia,
Alabama, and Mississippi. After several days of free and harmoni-
ous interchange of opinions, the group adopted a set of resolutions to guide them for the duration of the war.[8] These resolutions
were of the utmost importance to Vance, and he eagerly sought
to have the General Assembly approve them.

Endeavoring to clarify the various resolutions, he considered
first the one making it the patriotic duty of each state to aid its
neighbor in case of invasion or subjugation. This, he explained,
should be done only when a neighboring state had been invaded,
and if a state's best defensive point lay within the neighboring
state.[9]

The resolution that had aroused most interest and attention
throughout the state dealt with the impressment and conscription
of slaves. The *Weekly Standard,* along with other newspapers, considered it an effort to arm the slaves for military service, and
strongly expressed its aversion to the proposal. Answering this
attack on the resolution, Vance declared that it was not intended
to include the arming of slaves or their emancipation. Instead, he
contended, the Negro as any other person should be available to
the government for service in place of the able bodied white man
who could carry a musket. He disavowed completely any desire
to arm or emancipate the Negro:

Under no circumstances would I consent to see them armed, which
I would regard as not only dangerous in the extreme, but as less de-
grading only than their employment in this capacity by our enemies.
... This course would, it seems to me, surrender the entire question

which has ever separated the North from the South, would stultify ourselves in the eyes of the world, and render our whole revolution nugatory — a mere objectless waste of human life. . . . Our independence, I imagine, is chiefly desirable for the preservation of our great political institution; the principal of which is slavery, and it is only to be won by the blood of white freeman.[10]

The peroration of Vance's message was designed to reestablish his prestige with the people. He ended by commending North Carolinians for the good sense and conservatism exhibited in rescuing the state from the ruin of securing a separate peace. Stating that the unanimity at the polls had alleviated all apprehension regarding North Carolina's desertion of the rest of the South, Vance concluded that " a nobler moral spectacle has seldom been exhibited."[11]

At the time of the delivery of this message, the lawmakers were little concerned with Lee's dwindling army and dangerously thin line around Petersburg. Their chief interest lay in the defense of North Carolina.[12] Fort Fisher, located at the mouth of the Cape Fear River, served as the defense of the port of Wilmington, the chief source of supplies for Lee's army. Eager to eliminate this important supply center, the Union forces were intent upon capturing both Fort Fisher and Wilmington by the end of the year.

Vance was cognizant of the havoc which would be brought by these Union successes in North Carolina, and he appealed to every man who had "a spirit of a freeman in his bosom, a spark of fire or a drop of blood of heroes" to come to the rescue. "Your Governor," he said, "will meet you at the front and will share with you the worst."[13]

Vance delayed his departure for the front a few days, however, in order to deliver his second inaugural address. Since defeat was now inevitable, he was unable to offer the people much hope of success, but, along with other supporters of the Confederacy, he was still unwilling to openly admit failure. Nevertheless, he no longer talked of victory with the assurance of his earlier speeches, but calmly promised that "the thing that has been is the thing

that shall be." He neither made any new promises nor laid down
any new regulations.[14]

Lacking a clearly defined thesis, his inaugural address failed to
meet the standards of a well organized speech. He warned the people that the greatest danger to the South lay in disunion, distrac-
tion, and division of sentiments; and the greatest enemy of the
country was the individual who would "foment passion toward
internal violence and self destruction."[15] Following this admonish-
ment, the speech ended with this plea:

> Let all of our movement whether of peace or war be in solid columns
> — our people at home as our brothers at the front — standing in line
> and facing one way and together! Then victory is not only doubly
> offered but thrice glorious and defeat will be robbed of half its calam-
> ities.[16]

Vance's second inaugural address did little toward brightening
the darkened spirits of the people. With the fall of Atlanta and
the desperate straits of Lee's defenses around Petersburg, all hope
of success had now vanished. The federal fleet continued to pound
at Fort Fisher in an effort to bring a speedy termination of the
war by cutting off this valuable source of Confederate supplies.
The Confederate defenses there collapsed on January 15, 1865,
and Wilmington was occupied by federal troops following the fall
of Fort Fisher.[17] With this disaster came news of the failure of
the Confederate peace commission and the unchecked advance of
Sherman's army northward from Savannah.[18] The fears of North
Carolinians were further augmented by the knowledge that Sherman was advancing at the rate of eight miles a day, leaving desolation in his path.[19]

In an effort to console the people, on February 14, Vance issued
a proclamation. He pointed out that the Confederacy still possessed vast resources in men and supplies. If the people would
support the army, he declared, the South could still win the war.
Appealing to fear, he vividly presented the horrors that would
accompany defeat — four million slaves set free; lands confiscated;

women, children, and old men reduced to beggary; the gallows groaning under the burden of southern leaders. "Great God," Vance exclaimed, "is there a man in all this honorable, high spirited and noble commonwealth, so steeped in every conceivable meaness, so blackened with all the guilt of treason, or so damned with all the leprosy of cowardice, as to say, yes, we will submit to all this!"[20]

The Governor's proclamation apparently had little effect upon the people, for only ten days later Lee wrote to Vance urging him to do something to encourage public confidence and to dispel the feeling of despair among his people.[21] Acceding to Lee's request, Vance made a trip to the front lines, where he encouraged the men who were preparing to defend North Carolina from the powerful onslaught of the approaching Union forces.

On his way back to Raleigh, he stopped in Goldsboro on February 18, and made a speech in an effort to encourage the large crowd gathered to hear him. Hoping to cheer the people, he minimized the losses of the Confederacy and assured them of Lee's promise that Sherman must and would be stopped. After giving a vivid description of the patriotism that existed at the beginning of the war, he inquired, "How is it now when we begin to talk of battles not in Virginia, or Georgia or South Carolina, but in North Carolina?" He exhorted, "Now is the time to show if we have any backbone — to show if we are kin to the men who fought at Manassas or Gettysburg." Boasting of his own record of patriotism, he tried to instill the same patriotic spirit into the people by means of ethical persuasion. He said that he was one of the last to forsake the Union, but since his state had withdrawn from the Union forever he was ready to die for the pledges that were made there. "Are you?" he asked.[22]

Continuing his speech, Vance relied upon pathetic appeals to motivate his audience. In the following passage he described the dire consequences of submission as he appealed to the basic wants of self-preservation, preservation of ego, preservation of wealth, and altruism:

Four millions of slaves, a large number who are already armed, cast loose in our midst; our lands confiscated and sold out to pay the cost of subjugation and divided among negro soldiers as award for the slaughter of their masters; our women, men and children reduced to beggary, and cast out from our happy homes; our mutilated and diseased soldiers starving in rags from door to door, spurned by pensioned negro soldiers whilst the gallows grow weary under the burden of our wisest statesmen and bravest defenders; universal financial ruin and intolerable oppression and all of this because you were true to your country.[23]

Knowing that all good Southerners admired and respected Robert E. Lee, Vance capitalized on this sentiment as another source of appeal. In an emotionally packed sentence, he pictured "General Lee, the greatest captain of the age" bowing at the footstool of a low blackguard Illinois crossroads lawyer, to beg his life for the sake of his wife and children. "Are there any men in North Carolina," he asked, "willing to see this?" With cries of "Never! Never!" coming from the audience, he was assured that it was no longer apathetic. This audience reaction encouraged him to denounce those who would sanction such a degraded peace:

If there be, then there are no words in the lexicon I use capable of depicting the base brutality of his soul. No sirs, we mean to resist such demands. To submit is not better than the extremest resistance, and he who submits is a mean dog.[24]

Despite the darkness of the times, Vance sought in the speech to encourage the people. He told them that if they stood by the army and the government, he saw "in letters of living light, written upon tattered bloodstained banners the independence of the Confederate States in less than twelve months."[25] This was apparently an effort to cheer the people rather than a true expression of his belief for he wrote to Governor Brown of Georgia on January 18, *1865* "I regard it our chief aim at this time to hold the demoralized and trembling fragments of society and law together and prevent them from dropping to pieces until the rapidly hastening end of our struggle shall be developed."[26] Nevertheless, he maintained throughout the Goldsboro speech that prospects were not too gloomy. He had been encouraged, he claimed, by his visit a few days earlier with the soldiers at Wilmington. After talking to the men of General Hoke's lines, he was convinced that they were steadfast in their willingness to fight to the bitter end. His description of the attitude of these soldiers was one of the strongest appeals in the speech:

The common expression [of the soldiers] was 'Governor you take care of our folks at home as best you can, we'll fight this thing out yet. . . .' that is the voice of the brave fellows I saw there half clad and badly fed, standing many of them knee deep in the mud, their musket firmly clutched and their eyes bright and clear, firmly bent upon the foe some fifty to seventy yards in front.[27]

In the peroration of his last public speech as war governor, he attempted to emphasize the optimistic note of the body of the speech and to motivate the audience to cooperate vigorously in the war effort. "All we have to do is to stand firm together," he said, "to trust in Divine aid, but at the same time to do our duty by keeping an eye on human means."[28] Those who could do nothing better should cheer each other, and those who had the means should feed the families of the soldiers. "If you do not," declared Vance, "the land on which last year you raised such large crops will be plowed this year by the foe."[29]

Although Sherman's army was advancing through the southern counties of the state, Vance remained unwilling for North Carolina to initiate a movement that would lead to the surrender of the Confederacy. His friends as well as his political opponents were now advocating separate state action. Shortly after the failure of the Hampton Roads Conference, Senator William A. Graham appealed to Vance on behalf of a number of Confederate senators and representatives who were ready to concede defeat. In great secrecy, Graham asked Vance to issue an order for all North Carolina troops to return home in order to force Lee to surrender. Vance excitedly jumped from his seat and demanded to know if

Graham advised such action. "No," Graham answered, "I only deliver the message I was requested to bring." Vance then swore and angrily exclaimed:

No! I would see the last one of them in perdition before I would do it. Were I to do that, the last of it would not be heard for generations to come. It would be charged that the Confederacy might have succeeded but for the treachery of North Carolina. So far as the honor of the state is in my keeping it shall be untarnished. She must stand or fall with her sisters.[30]

Convinced that total collapse of the Confederacy was inevitable, on April 12 Vance sent Graham and Swain to Sherman at Goldsboro, with a flag of truce. Along with verbal instructions to learn on what terms Vance could remain in Raleigh to conduct the functions of his office, they carried a letter requesting an interview with Sherman.[31]

Although the commissioners planned to return to Raleigh by four o'clock in the afternoon, Sherman was determined that they should remain at his camp until the next morning. He suggested that the engine of their train needed repairs, and promised that the train would be at their service as soon as the repairs were made.[32] Why Sherman wanted to delay the return of the commissioners is not known, but whatever the reason, they were detained at a crucial time. Sherman's men were expected to enter Raleigh during the night, and the Governor's action depended upon Sherman's reply to his letter.[33]

After having made arrangements to leave Raleigh, Vance eagerly waited until midnight for the commissioners' return. Unwilling to trust himself to Yankee hands, he then mounted his horse and rode out to where General Hoke and eight thousand North Carolinians were encamped. Here he slept the remainder of the night on a blanket in the general's tent, and left on the morning of April 13 for Hillsboro where he hoped to meet Graham and Swain. Although the commissioners had not arrived in Hillsboro, Vance spent the night at Graham's home where the two commissioners found him the next morning and delivered Sherman's reply.[34]

Vance hoped to resume his duties as governor, but he first responded to a request to meet President Davis in Greensboro. Upon his arrival in Greensboro, however, he found that the President and his cabinet had moved on to Charlotte. Consequently, he followed them there. Arriving in Charlotte, he met with Davis and his cabinet. Davis was optimistic as he discussed the status of the Confederacy. He urged Vance to assist in retreating beyond the Mississippi with the soldiers who were still faithful to the Confederate cause. Upon the completion of his remarks a long silence followed. This was finally broken by John C. Breckinridge, a member of the cabinet, who declared that Mr. Davis was not speaking candidly to Governor Vance, and that he should not be advised to forsake the duties of office to follow a retreating Confederacy. "Well," replied Davis, "perhaps, General, you are right." Agreeing with Breckinridge, Vance shook hands with the President and bade farewell to the Confederacy.[35]

Vance's desire to return to his official duties never was realized, however, for the Confederate military authorities would not allow him to pass through the lines while negotiations between General Sherman and General Johnston were in progress.[36] Although negotiations soon ended in a treaty which would have meant the recognition of state governments and the avoidance of the humiliation and ruin of Reconstruction, the federal government refused to approve it.[37] General Schofield was placed in charge of Raleigh, and he refused to allow Vance to return to the Capitol.[38]

In an effort to avert some of the distress confronting the people, Vance issued his last proclamation on April 28. He urged the people to abstain from all lawlessness, and called upon the soldiers to organize into groups and arrest or slay "any bodies of lawless and unauthorized men who may be committing depredations upon the persons or property of peaceable citizens. . . ."[39]

After issuing this proclamation, Vance remained in Greensboro until the arrival of General Schofield. He surrendered himself to Schofield, who refused to arrest him because he had no orders from the federal government. Instead, he was told to go to his

family in Statesville.[40] Gathering together his few remaining pos-
sessions, consisting of a saddle horse, a wagon, and a pair of mules,
Vance placed them in a freight car to travel with him to Statesville, where he arrived on April 14. His wife and four sons had
taken refuge there before Sherman's march on Raleigh, and there
the family remained until Vance was arrested by a detachment of
soldiers on May 13, his thirty-fifth birthday.

On May 14, Vance left Statesville for Salisbury and leaving
Salisbury on May 15, he arrived in Washington on May 20, and
was immediately placed in the Old Capitol prison, where he remained for forty-seven days.[41] W. W. Holden, who had been appointed governor to replace Vance, was urged by one of Vance's
friends to ask President Johnson to release him so he could return
to his wife who was seriously ill.[42] Johnson released Vance immediately upon receipt of Holden's letter, and he arrived home
on July 6.

CHAPTER VI

POST-WAR SPEAKING, 1865-1876

After he joined his wife and sons at his home in Statesville in August, 1865, Vance's chief concern was to find some way to earn a living. Friends immediately began efforts to establish him in a law practice, and for a time it seemed that through their efforts he might settle in Wilmington.[1] A visit to Charlotte, however, resulted in an offer to form a law partnership with Clement Dowd and R. D. Johnson.[2] The attractiveness of this offer, together with the detrimental effects that Wilmington's coastal climate might have on his wife's health, determined his decision to settle in Charlotte.[3] On April 3, 1866, the Charlotte *Western Democrat* announced that Z. B. Vance, C. D. Dowd, and R. D. Johnston would practice law together.

As a young lawyer Vance had allowed his hair to grow long enough to curl at the end, as was the style with southern politicians and lawyers. During the war, however, he had had it cut short. Now letting his hair grow long again, he donned a low collar and string tie, and hit the circuit. He found that he had forgotten many principles of law since he had last practiced, and recognizing this weakness he told Dowd, "Every law office contains one working man and one gentleman. In this partnership, I propose to be the gentleman." Thus it was arranged for Dowd to prepare the cases and Vance to deliver the speeches to the juries.

Vance's trial speeches became gala occasions. Crowds poured into the courtroom when he was scheduled to speak, for they were assured of good entertainment. Even the ladies, who usually considered it improper to attend court, came in numbers.[4]

Vance was probably better able to sway juries than any other lawyer in the state. This unusual power may be attributed in part to his understanding of practical psychology. He was familiar with basic motives which move audiences to attention and action. Keeping his eyes on the jury while he spoke, he observed their reaction, and was quick to adapt his speech to it. The jurors almost unconsciously accepted his views, which were well supported by facts, arranged in compact arguments, and interspersed with apt and humorous illustrations.[5] According to Judge David Schenck, who presided over some of the cases in which Vance appeared, he was "an orator of unexampled power both in the power of his imagination and the force of his language; he handles pathos with delicate tenderness and wields the fierceness of satire with piercing sharpness. But as a humorist he has no equal, perhaps on the continent."[6]

Vance created a problem for the judges, especially the more serious ones. During some cases, it was practically impossible to preserve order in the courtroom while he was speaking.

Although Vance was successful in influencing juries, he did not enjoy the practice of law. This may, perhaps, be attributed to his meager legal training. He only used the profession to make a living while he was outside the political arena.[7] Making the best of the situation, however, he took pains to make his courtroom speaking interesting for himself and others. There is no record that he ever practiced before the State Supreme Court; evidently, he preferred to remain in the less formal county courts.[8]

Soon after he began his law practice in Charlotte, local communities began clamoring for him to deliver public addresses. Fearful that what he might say would jeopardize his chances for a pardon, he was reluctant to speak. On July 26, 1867, he wrote Swain, "I am beset on all sides to make speeches, or write for the papers, etc., but for fear of doing harm I have remained quiet."[9]

A year earlier, however, he made one exception and consented to deliver a lecture on June 7, 1866, before the two literary societies during commencement at the University of North Carolina.

Vance's advice to the audience, which included the three graduates of the university for the year, was both wise and timely. He
spoke on "The Duties of Defeat," calling for "a sincere acceptance
of the decisions of the war, loyalty to our governments, national
and state, faithful labor for the reconstruction of society, for the
upbuilding of the material interests of our people and education
of our children."[10]

In spite of Vance's irritation with the conditions produced by
Reconstruction, he used good judgment and exhibited no bitterness as he spoke. His lecture demonstrated a workmanship that
was often lacking in his speeches. Although he claimed insufficient
time as the reason for his hesitancy in permitting the lecture to be
published, one must conclude from the quality of the finished
product that he made good use of what time he had.

The introduction to the lecture was designed to interest and
secure the attention of the audience from the first utterance. Using
an analogy, Vance helped the audience feel the emotions of one
approaching the university for the first time since the war. He
began:

As the traveler, who during his absence, has learned that a great
fire has swept over his native city, welcomes with the keenest rapture
the first glance of his own home, which he trembles at the thought of
finding in the ashes of the general ruin, so should we rejoice to be-
hold our honored university surviving the wreck of so much that we
loved and revered — Though staggering under the blows of adversity,
I am so happy to see for myself, this day, a goodly display of her
ancient life and energy.[11]

No man was more aware than Vance of the calamities that had
imperiled the state. With these in mind, he explained in the style
of the typical commencement address that the graduates were
entering the duties of life under physical and social conditions
unique in the history of their country. His description of these
conditions is a concise and vivid picture of the desolation left by
the war.

With her homesteads burned to ashes, with fields desolated, with thousands of her noblest and bravest children sleeping in beds of slaughter;

innumerable orphans, widows, and helpless persons reduced to beggary and deprived of their natural protectors; her corporations bankrupt and her own credit gone; her public charities overthrown, her educational fund utterly lost, her land filled from end to end with her maimed and mutilated soldiers; denied all representation in the public counsels, her heart-broken and wretched people are not only oppressed with the weight of their own indebtedness, but are crushed into the very dust by taxation for the mighty debt incurred as the cost of their own subjugation![12]

This dark picture, said Vance, was not presented to cause the young men to despair, but rather as a challenge to inspire them to rebuild their fallen state. Expressing a firm belief that the "bloody footprints of ruthless war" could be erased by intelligent industry, Vance said:

Looking despairingly at the condition of things, the country turns toward her young men and calls to them to lead the way in preaching and practicing hope. You are required, above all things, to teach our people to look up from the crumbling ashes and prostrate columns of their present ruin, to the majestic proportions and surpassing grandeur of that temple which may yet be built by the hand which labors, the mind which conceives, and the great soul which faints not.[13]

A knowledge of his loyal devotion to the Union and opposition to secession before the war go far toward vindicating him from an accusation of insincerity in uttering the following words:

The best test of the best heroism, now, is a cheerful and loyal submission to the powers and events established in our defeat, and a ready obedience to the Constitution and laws of the country.[14]

The organization of the speech was good. The body was clearly delineated from the introduction and conclusion. The introduction, presenting existing conditions with a challenge to work for the state's recovery, was followed by the body which outlined specific duties to be performed. Then came the conclusion, which was an epitome of the speech as a whole. Thus, the entire lecture adhered closely to its subject and purpose.

Continuing the lecture, Vance explained that each side had been grievously deceived in its estimate of the other during the war. Now the North was again deceived, he contended, into believing the South would find difficulty in arising from its stricken status. He said:

> It will be our duty now ... to undeceive them by the vigor and energy with which we shall clear away the wreck of our fallen fortunes, adapt ourselves to circumstances under changed institutions and new systems of labor, and the rapidity with which we shall travel in those ways which lead to the rebuilding and adorning a state.[15]

The second duty resting upon youthful citizens, Vance continued, was "looking after and caring for the orphans of those who perished in your defense and mine." He believed the moral as well as the physical welfare of these orphans should be the concern of all the people. Explaining that the public school system had collapsed with the war and the loss of the literary fund, he claimed that little remained to prevent the moral decay of young people. To illustrate this point, Vance told of a soldier's orphaned son who was brought into court to account for crimes committed because he lacked the bare necessities of life and any parental supervision.[16]

But the duties of defeat, Vance declared, did not end with showing concern for the soldier's children. Honor should also be accorded the war dead. This plea was in furtherance of his policy as war governor, in which he sought to provide for the soldiers. Now there was one last thing that must be done for those who had died in battle; this he expressed as the third duty of defeat:

> We owe to the dead what it is possible to do for their remains and their memories, and charge of faithlessness to our own obligations, it seems to me, should stand between us and its discharge.
> 'Their bones are scattered far and wide
> By mount, by stream and sea,'
> and it is not for the purpose of eulogizing the cause, for which they perished, that we would gather them up for decent sepulture, and perpetuate their memories by tables of stone.[17]

Looking toward the return of representative government, Vance said, "The time is not far distant when as citizens, I trust, you will be permitted to take a part in the government of your country." When that time came, there would be one further duty for all to perform:

... it is our country still, and if it cannot be governed as we wish it, it must be governed some other way; and it is still our duty to labor for its prosperity and glory, with ardor and sincerity. I earnestly urge upon you the strictest conformity of your conduct to the situation; to what the government actually is, not what you may think it ought to be.[18]

After President Johnson granted him a pardon on March 11, 1867,[19] he lectured more frequently. This added to his meager income, although many lectures were delivered gratis or with the proceeds going for some charitable purpose. Soon the Tar Heel spokesman was appearing in large lecture halls in Baltimore, Philadelphia, and New Orleans. He was speaking at county fairs, to historical societies, boards of trade, and graduating classes. By the early 1870's, his national reputation as a lecturer was firmly established.[20]

On February 13, 1874, he spoke at the Masonic Temple in Baltimore. So far as available records show, this was the first presentation of his famous lecture, the "Scattered Nation." This lecture, which will be treated extensively in a later chapter of this study, was delivered in almost every important city in the United States.[21]

Apparently the only lecture of the period that caused any controversy was Vance's address before the Southern Historical Society at White Sulphur Springs, Virginia, in August, 1875. He spoke on North Carolina's role in the Civil War, and offered a bit of secret history to show that there was "faintness of heart and smiting together of the knees in parts of the South other than North Carolina." In the closing days of the war, he said, W. A. Graham, who was then a Confederate senator, visited him on behalf of certain gentlemen in Richmond, urging Vance "to take steps for making terms with Mr. Lincoln and thus inaugurate the conclusion" of the war. Graham said he had agreed to lay the request before Vance, but had not promised to add his personal advice. When asked for the names of the men making the request, Graham gave them. The majority were Confederate senators and representatives. Of course, Vance declined the proposition, and "asked Graham to say to these gentlemen, with my compliments, that in the mountains of North Carolina, where I was reared, when a man was whipped he had to do his own hallooing, that the technical word, enough, could not be cried by proxy."[22]

Vance's lecturing was more than a way of earning money. It gave him an opportunity to show his intense interest in the political affairs of the state. It was impossible for Vance to be an idle spectator during the ominous days of Reconstruction. Although he was unable to hold office, he played a significant role in wresting control of the government from the Radicals.

A constitutional convention met in Raleigh on January 14, 1868. Only thirteen Conservatives were present. The Republicans numbered 107—18 carpetbaggers, 15 Negroes, and 74 native whites. This group adopted a new constitution, with many changes that showed the influence of the northern element in the convention. Yet, in general, it was a sound document. Indeed, it was "so modern and democratic that with some changes it has remained effective to this day."[88]

While the constitutional convention controlled by the Radicals—the term applied to the Republicans—was meeting in the state capitol, the Conservatives were also in Raleigh holding a convention of their own in Tucker Hall. Early in the meeting of the Conservatives Vance arose and responded to the calls for him to speak. He began his remarks in his characteristically humorous manner. He told of an Irishman who was looking at a donkey engine used in unloading ships. Gazing at it for awhile, he exclaimed: "Arrah, ye may puff and smoke and smoke and rattle away, tell ye' clane out of breath, and do the work of twenty men

at that, but blast ye, ye can't vote."[23] In keeping with his habit of always relating his stories to the idea he was presenting, he added:

So Mr. Chairman, I may puff and smoke, but I can't vote for all of that. Still sir, though, I may be deprived of all political power in the land of my affections and nativity. Yet I can still claim to be a white man.[24]

As this statement indicates, the actions of Holden and the other white Republican leaders were obnoxious to Vance. He was galled at the establishment of unqualified Negro suffrage, while many patriotic and loyal citizens, including himself, were deprived of political rights. This resentment found further expression in scathing, sarcastic remarks:

. . . and what is more, I have no prejudices against my own color. I may add that I have none against the black race. They have behaved well in the past and whenever they had gone astray, it has been almost invariably at the instigation of some white rascal.[25]

There was little the Conservative convention could do other than protest against the policies of the state and national governments and nominate candidates to be defeated in the coming election. Its principal accomplishment was the adoption of a set of resolutions setting forth the philosophy of the Conservative party. These resolutions pronounced unalterable devotion to the federal Constitution, protested against the Reconstruction acts, opposed the political and social equality of Negroes, and approved President Johnson's efforts toward Reconstruction.

After an enthusiastic endorsement of these resolutions, the crowd clamored for Vance to speak again. He responded by saying that he had nothing to add because his theme was fully exhausted. "If there was any man in the state," he said, "outside of the Insane Asylum, who needed any argument to convince him that the white man must rule this country, life was too short for him to waste breath on him."

As Vance continued to speak, he reminded the audience that only a few Conservatives had voted even when they had the chance. When the decision for a constitutional convention rested with the people, many did not vote although they were opposed to it. Believing that it was the duty of all honest white citizens to exercise this prerogative, he produced one of the most persuasive efforts of his speaking career. He said:

Our timidity, heretofore, has been lamentable. With 30,000 majority in the state, the white people allowed the recent election to go by default, when ordinary spirit and exertion would have secured them ascendancy and victory. How can you claim to be free men, if you are willing for fear of losing a little remnant of property, to submit to the control of 70,000 negroes, marshaled to the meanest white men whom God had ever made? If with the power in your hands, you cravenly yield to such control, how can you stand the comparison with the good and noble men of our illustrous North Carolina past? How can you stand the comparison with your own boys, who taking their lives in their hands, bravely bared their bosoms, in the late war to the shock of battle for the land of their nativity and affections.[26]

Having thus appealed to pride, he turned his appeal to the motive of self-preservation. The preservation of the white race was his concern as he questioned:

What are you afraid of? Confiscation? Why half of us now can't begin to pay our debts. Bayonets? Why we have been living among them for years. Military law? Why the sacred muniment of Habeas Corpus has grown so rusty that the best lawyers in the country have to read up to know what it means. There is something of which you may well be afraid. Better be afraid of what lies before you—of leaving a heritage of servitude to your children and children's children.[27]

As a result of his convention speeches, Vance re-established himself as the political leader of the Conservatives. The *Raleigh Sentinel* reported that after he had finished speaking, "the delights of the audience knew no bounds, on the floors and in the galleries, the people vented themselves in unrestrained applause."[28]

Before the adjournment of the convention, a resolution was passed authorizing the executive committee to call another convention. The members met in Raleigh on February 28, and nominated Vance as the Conservative candidate for governor and Colonel E. D. Hill for lieutenant governor.[29]

Despite the esteem in which he was held by the Conservatives, Vance saw the handwriting on the wall. He was aware that a Conservative could not be elected. There were only 117,428 white people registered, as against 79,444 Negroes. With all of the Negroes and the white Republicans voting the Republican ticket, the Conservative-Democrats would not have a chance. Consequently, Vance wrote the committee on March 6, "After mature reflection, both by public and private considerations, I reluctantly decline the nomination."[30] Thomas A. Ashe was then chosen to replace Vance on the ticket.[31]

The Democratic National Convention was held in New York, July 3-10, 1868. Vance attended as a delegate representing the Conservative party of North Carolina. While there he made several speeches, but only one of them received any recognition. This one is usually labeled his Union Square speech. It was probably delivered at a demonstration meeting of the Metropolitan Club, held on July 9 at the St. Augustine House near Union Square to celebrate the nominations of Horatio Seymour for president of the United States and Frank Blair for vice-president. The speech was used by Vance to express in a satirical manner his strong dislike of the North's forcing Negro suffrage on the South. Using his own brand of doggerel verse, he characterized the attitude of the New Englander:

> To every Southern River shall Negro suffrage come
> But not to fair New England for that's too close to hum.

With an accusing finger pointed at the North, he declared:

They preferred Negro suffrage at long range. If they could have the Negro vote in South Carolina, all well; but in Michigan, New York and the other northern and western states they declined him favor.[32]

During the next two years Vance, as well as all other opponents of the Radicals, was anxiously awaiting a collapse of the government.

The power of the Conservatives had increased considerably when the General Assembly reconvened in the fall of 1869, and in 1870 the Conservatives elected five of seven representatives to Congress and captured both houses of the General Assembly. With the control of the legislature in the hands of the Conservatives, Holden was doomed.

When the General Assembly convened on November 21, 1870, "the roll call revealed that the voice of an indignant and outraged people had ejected most of the robbers from the legislature and replaced them with familiar names of patriotic North Carolinians."[33] On November 29, Vance was elected to the United States Senate by both houses of the General Assembly.

After his election, a large number of friends serenaded Vance at the Exchange Hotel where he was staying in Raleigh. Responding in a speech that was well adapted to the occasion, he advocated moderation and denounced "the vicious and vindicative of all sorts."

Now that we have the government of North Carolina in our hands, we should not aim to avenge ourselves for the overriding of civil liberty among us, but we should so arrange that it cannot happen again—should see to it that no executive or other authority can again attempt to destroy our liberties. . . . Let anger, revenge and retaliation be ignored, and let the laws on your statute books bear the impress of a free people determined legitimately to maintain their freedom. In my place in the Senate I shall endeavor to serve my great state and country with honor. Every law both state and national should be respected and obeyed by all our people, bitterness and vituperation should cease, and men no longer endeavoring to destroy each other should earnestly strive to engender kindly feelings among all classes of our citizens. To bring about these desirable ends will be the earnest aim of my life in Congress and elsewhere.[34]

The General Assembly brought charges against Holden. After a month-long trial, he was convicted on six or eight charges, and became the first governor of the state to be removed from office by impeachment. Vance's comment was: "It was the longest hunt after the poorest hide I ever saw."[35]

Vance was scheduled to take his seat in the Senate on March 5, 1871, but that body refused to admit him. The House had passed an amnesty bill that would have allowed Vance to take the seat to which he was unquestionably elected, but when it reached the Senate, Joseph C. Abbott, his predecessor, had an amendment attached to the bill which excluded Vance.[36]

Exactly one year after his election to the Senate, Vance submitted his resignation, since his disabilities had not been removed. Matt W. Ransom was then elected to take his place. Ransom had been in the Senate only a short time before he succeeded in having this done, however, and at last Vance was free to participate in politics at will. When the Democratic convention met in Greensboro on May 1, 1872, it was charged with the responsibility of selecting a candidate for governor. The leaders wanted Vance, but Vance declined to run, and could not be persuaded by their pleas. Why he refused is not definitely known, but it is probable that he was interested in the Senate seat that would be vacant in the fall. Augustus Merrimon then became the gubernatorial candidate, with the promise that in case of defeat he would receive the nomination for the Senate vacancy.[37]

While waiting for the next political opportunity, Vance became engaged in civic affairs. The papers carried accounts of his acting as master of ceremonies at concerts,[38] as chairman for a public lecture,[39] and giving a speech to a group of townspeople gathered at the local grandstand.[40]

On June 14, 1876, the Democrats held their convention in Raleigh, and nominated the man who could make the best race for governor, "Zebulon B. Vance, famous orator, superb stump speaker, popular war governor, and champion of state rights."[41]

CHAPTER VII

THE VANCE-SETTLE CAMPAIGN

The news of Vance's nomination was received with approval all over the state. At Charlotte, where he had lived for the past ten years, a self-appointed committee began making plans for a celebration upon Vance's return from the convention. Handbills announcing a meeting to be held in Independence Square were printed and distributed throughout the city. Long before the arrival of the 9:20 p.m. train, which was bringing Vance from Raleigh, tar barrels were set on fire and throngs of people gathered in the streets waiting to hear what their distinguished townsman had to say about his nomination. A large delegation was waiting at the depot when the train pulled in, and the popular candidate was hurried into a waiting carriage, which was pulled by four grey horses to the Square. As the carriage came in sight a band began playing, and shouts of "hurrah for Vance" echoed through the air.[1]

Amid thunderous applause, Vance mounted the platform which was illuminated by blazing tar barrels. He was introduced to the crowd as "North Carolina's favorite son, the tribune of the people, Zebulon B. Vance."

Speaking for only fifteen minutes, Vance explained that his remarks would be brief because he was exhausted from the activities of the convention. He had had little rest since he had left home three days earlier because of "the continued evidences of partiality and kindnesses shown by his fellow citizens."[2] Optimistically he declared that victory for the Democrats was presaged on every hand. The convention had had the largest attendance of any ever held in the state and all who attended were strong supporters of the Democratic ticket. Even cautious men and women, Vance said, were predicting that the Democrats would carry the state by a twenty thousand vote majority.[3]

The most important reason for expecting success was that the people were aroused, and wanted a change from the type of government that had existed for the past sixteen years. Establishing himself as the man ethically equipped to carry out a reform platform, Vance avowed:

I can lift up these hands before you, in the presence of my Creator, and say that in all that time of war and public distress, and through all that period of temptation and corruption which followed the war, not one dollar of dishonest money has ever stained their palms; and, lastly I can say that I never thought wherein self was preferred to prosperity and honor of my native land.[4]

honest

Ready for the opening of the campaign, Vance arrived in Raleigh on July 13. That night four hundred members of the Tilden-Vance Club, headed by a brass band, marched from their meeting hall to the Yarbrough House, where Vance was staying, to serenade him. Amid much cheering, Vance appeared on the portico and gave a brief preview of the campaign. Declaring that the struggle would be long and exciting, he promised that if it were not pleasant and genteel, it would be no fault of his.[5]

At the time of this speech, native white Republicans were becoming exasperated with the conduct of their own party, and a general exodus had already begun. Even two Grant electors of 1872 stumped the state for Tilden.[6] Recognizing this dissatisfaction, Vance tried to appeal to the Republicans in the hope of gaining their vote. He said that he had no quarrel with the great mass of Republicans, black or white, but with their corrupt leaders he did have a quarrel. He intended, therefore, "to lash them from every stump, fearlessly."[7] He promised to tell the people of an appalling tale of corruption in the administration of affairs during the Reconstruction years. With the stage thus set, Vance bade his admirers good night, and promised that they should hear more from him the next day and for many days to come.[8]

A little after eleven o'clock the next morning Vance, accompanied by W. R. Cox, chairman of the Democratic Executive Committee, mounted the large flag-draped platform, which had been built in the courthouse square. All of the thousand seats facing the platform were taken, and an overflow crowd swelled through the square. Vance's appearance was greeted by a wild demonstration and he was bubbling over with exuberance by the time he reached the platform. He was introduced as the man "in whom centered all reform, reconciliation and union" in North Carolina.

In beginning his address, he tried to establish goodwill by assuring the audience that he was thoroughly familiar with the duties of the office he sought. He explained that during the dark and troubled time of the war he had been responsible for enforcing many harsh laws, but that they were as unpleasant to him as to those against whom they were enforced.

He promised to state his views frankly and honestly. Although the war had ended, Vance said, there were many vital issues still to be settled. Chief among these was the question of the supremacy of the white race, a policy which he strongly affirmed. His argument that the achievements of the Anglo-Saxon race had earned it the right to supremacy wherever Christianity and civilization prevailed may have lacked logic, but it was strong in appeal to the prejudices of the great mass of white voters. In all sincerity, Vance said, he believed in the doctrine he preached, and declared that "this supremacy would never pass to alien blood with his consent."[9]

Judge Thomas Settle, his opponent in the race, had sent Vance a note fifteen minutes before he left his hotel, and Vance agreed to open with an hour speech and let Settle speak for one and one-half hours, after which Vance would close with a speech of the same length. This was the procedure that the Republican party had used with the Democrats in the campaign of 1868. Settle, however, refused to debate Vance on these terms. Commenting on the refusal, Vance vividly expressed his point in figurative language that was familiar to all the audience. "I fed them," he said, "out of their own spoon, but they did not seem to like the victuals."[10]

This remark illustrates Vance's inimitable mode of changing uninteresting material into a captivating idea by his free and easy use of figures of speech.

In its denunciation of the villanies and inconsistences of the Reconstruction Acts, Vance's speech of July 14 set a pattern for his other speeches of the campaign. He argued that throughout the ten years of Reconstruction, Congress had dissolved the Union that it professedly wanted to preserve. By this argument he sought to expose what he believed to be the fallacy in the conduct of the federal government. It fought to keep the southern states from leaving the Union, but as soon as the South was defeated, Congress declared them out of the Union and would not let them re-enter until they had met certain prescribed conditions. Vance contended that the North Carolina convention which had written the new state constitution was formed in violation of the federal constitution since many white people had been disfranchised. In support of this point, he reviewed Congressional procedure in obtaining a constitution that would satisfy the Radical Congress:

Congress ordained that the body should be convened, prescribed how members should be elected, and then proceeded to disfranchise 30,000 white men. Under this Congressional manipulation, a constitutional convention was called, a constitution framed, and 80,000 Negroes who had no right to vote voted upon the question of their own franchisement; 30,000 white men who had a right to vote were not allowed to vote on the question at all.[11]

In order to strengthen his argument, Vance used an analogy. He said that the action of Congress was "like fifteen men going to a church of twenty, applying for membership and insisting on voting on their own election, and then dis-franchising one-third of the original number, thus placing themselves in the majority and taking control."[12] Vance often used analogies, especially figurative analogies, to relate a less familiar point to one which was familiar. If Vance were not able to prove his point with his analogies, he used them to good advantage in clarifying his material. Doubtless much of his powerful audience appeal may be attributed to his skillful handling of the homely analogy.

From the very outset of the compaign Republican newspapers and candidates began to attack Vance. One charge, though sadistic in character, took a humorous twist under Vance's defense. He had been accused of having women's thumbs squeezed under fence rails to make them tell where their husbands were hiding. Denouncing the charge as an "infamous lie," he threatened that any man who would repeat this story to his face would be made to swallow the lie. He turned the tables on his accusers by his firm avowal that he had "never squeezed a woman by the thumbs or in any other way except by her permission."[13]

Disparaging his opponents indictments against him as "slanderous charges put into circulation by unscrupulous men,"[14] Vance asserted that nothing in his wartime administration was equal to the state of affairs in 1870. Then there had prevailed a state of turmoil "created by designing, bad and base men."[15] Governor Holden had had citizens arrested by both white and black soldiers, and had refused them the right of trial. To prove this assertion, Vance mentioned a Felix Roan and Lucien Murray as examples of men who had been arrested and tortured without writ of habeas corpus. They were accused of having knowledge of Ku Klux Klan activities in which a Negro and a Radical politician had been murdered. When Roan and Murray refused to admit knowledge of the affair, they were strung up until they were unconscious. Many were punished without being brought to trial. The state Supreme Court issued writs of habeas corpus, but Holden would not honor them. Then explained Vance:

The courts refused to force him to do so, and stood supinely by and saw some of our best citizens dragged to prison by a rabble soldiery without a proper warrant and some even put to torture, and refused to interpose the law.[16]

At this point Vance reached the climax of his speech by asking the rhetorical question, "Who was on the Supreme Court bench at the time?"[17] The answer, of course, was Thomas Settle. With this he completed his defense, and the charges of his being untrue to the people were not to be taken seriously again at any time during the campaign.

The speech made a greater use of logical proof than did the majority of Vance's political addresses. He also documented to a greater degree than usual the evidence used in this speech.

In accepting Settle's challenge to meet him in debate during the campaign, Vance had agreed to match his wits with the most formidable opponent of his career. Settle's learning in the law, his abundance of general information and political experience; and his skill in debate caused many of Vance's friends to fear the result. But in the qualities that make an orator, Vance was superior to Settle.

Although both Vance and Settle were handsome men, there was something majestic in Vance's appearance. He was nearly six feet tall, and weighed about 230 pounds. His chest was full and heavy, and his neck short and thick. Crowning his large well-shaped head was a mass of glossy black hair that grew well down on his forehead and temples on the right side, and receded excessively at the part on the left. Long locks of hair hung low on his neck. A large mustache curling at the corners adorned the upper lip.[18]

The first meeting of "the giants" took place before four thousand people at Rutherfordton on July 25. Vance opened the meeting with a 90-minute speech. Settle followed with one of the same length, and each replied for a half hour. The speakers set a high standard of conduct for the campaign by being courteous to each other. Vance with his cleverness, however, never missed an opportunity to upset his opponent. For example, in the first debate Settle read a letter he had procured from Vance's letter book, which was on file at the War Department. The letter advocated making desertion of the army a misdemeanor, and Settle chose to read only the parts that made Vance appear disloyal to the people of North Carolina. When Vance's turn came, he asked for the letter, held it up to the audience, and showed that in the reading much had been omitted. In a sarcastic voice he arraigned the federal government for denying him access to his own letter book, and attacked Settle for using "garbled copies against him."[19]

Vance was too intelligent to allow Settle's continuous attack on his war record to put him on the defensive. In fact, Vance had a barrage of questions which were designed to place Settle in a dilemma and to associate him with repulsive acts of the Republican party. The following questions were used in practically every debate:

1. Was Holden's suspension of the writ of habeas corpus legal?
2. Which of the constitutional amendments are good?
3. How did the South get out of the Union?
4. Were the reconstruction acts constitutional?
5. Can Congress confer the right of suffrage?
6. Was the Louisiana outrage constitutional?
7. Was Judge Settle not elected to the Supreme Court by fraud?
8. Does Judge Settle approve Grant's administration?
9. Does he approve of the civil rights act?
10. Was desertion from the army right?[20]

The first time these questions were used was at the little mountain town of Bakersville. The town had gone "all out" for the debate. The women had made campaign banners, and the largest crowd ever assembled in Mitchell County was present. Settle appealed to the prejudices of the people and opened old war wounds by a review of Vance's war record. Then Vance arose and said he had some questions to ask Mr. Settle. The ten questions were asked, but they were not satisfactorily answered. He said they reminded him "of the question if corn was fifty cents a bushel, and three pecks to a bushel, how much would it take to shingle a house?"

In a speech at Boone, Settle attempted to answer Vance on the question of whether he approved of Grant's administration. Settle said that the President himself confessed that he had made some blunders. In his opinion, however, Grant's administration would emblazon the pages of American history and shine by the side of George Washington's. This answer played into Vance's hand. He said that he didn't doubt the shine part, but suggested there was also a smell attached to it that resembled very much "the flavor of rotten mackerel in the sunshine."[21]

One of the liveliest discussions occurred at Jonesboro on August 25. Here the debate changed somewhat in character. Settle took a new approach in attacking Vance's war record. Instead of charging him with harshness toward conscripts and deserters, he held Vance responsible for extending a war which resulted in a loss of two-thirds of the property of the state. This charge referred to Vance's refusal to join Holden in the "peace movement" of 1863. He further attributed the loss of a $2,000,000 school fund to the fact that Vance had invested it in Confederate bonds. To avoid being put on the defensive, Vance did not clash directly on these issues. He sought to relegate all charges against his war record to the background with a blistering invective of the Republican leaders. He said that if he owned a full-blooded radical, he would trade him off for a dog and kill the dog. Treating the state revenue officers to similar insults, he characterized them as being able to "lie down and drink out of a branch and tell if there was a still five miles up it," or to "look at a man's track and tell whether he was toting a quart of whiskey or a two gallon jug."[22]

One of the issues of the campaign centered in the inconsistencies Vance and Settle had shown in their political affiliations. During the years preceding the outbreak of the war both had been Unionists, and were earnestly opposed to secession. In 1861, both were candidates for Congress and campaigned in their respective districts as anti-secessionists. During the campaign, however, both changed colors and became secessionists.[23] Vance charged Settle with "changing fronts and deserting the Confederate cause when the war got hot."

I will tell you the difference between Judge Settle and myself. I was a Union man at the beginning of the war and stuck to it until my state went out of the Union. I could not turn my gun against my own people, so I went with them and made the best fight I could. My competitor, Judge Settle, on the the other hand was a violent war man and was such a red hot secessionist that if you had thrown him into a branch he would have scalded to death every tadpole for a mile and a half below him.[24]

Settle's position became weaker as the debate continued. On August 18, at the little town of Danbury he lost control of his temper, interrupting Vance with, "That is not so." Vance had accused Settle of refusing to allow two men to serve in his company, while he was an army officer, because they were draftees rather than volunteers. He said that Settle drummed them from his company as cowards. Settle replied, "That is not so. No men were drummed from my company." Just then a man in the crowd stood up and shouted, "It is so, Captain Settle. I was there and I know the fact." Settle thinking about it, rejoined, "Yes, but not for cowardice, I had them drummed out for larceny." Vance marked up another point to his credit with the retort, "Would to God, fellow citizens, all the others, for larceny, could be drummed out of Captain Settle's company."[25]

Both candidates were heckled during the debates, but Vance was better able to cope with the situation than his opponent. In replying to Settle's charges regarding his treatment of deserters during the war, Vance declared he could never respect men who ran away from their colors. At that moment, a voice from the crowd interrupted, "Do you mean the conscripts that deserted?" "No," answered Vance, "I refer to men [who] volunteered and then deserted; of course, I have no reference to conscripts." "Well you ought to say," replied the voice. "My friend," said Vance, "please let us have it understood, I shall say exactly what I please." This quieted the heckler for the rest of the speech.[26]

Reaching the rural community of Johnson's Store on October 5, the candidates found a crowd of four thousand people gathered to hear them. For a mile on both sides of the road the thickets were full of horses, mules, and vehicles. The speaker's platform had been built in the woods to provide protection from the weather.

Perhaps the setting reminded Vance of a brush arbor camp meeting, for he adopted the style of the circuit preacher as he admonished his audience to pay no attention to Republican promises of reform. He said that these promises reminded him of the Dutchman who found it necessary to reform the sheep killing dog by cutting off a piece of his tail right behind his ears. At one point, he declared, "Reformation never began in Hell." At another, "The Devil never yet led a revival of religion." Using a Biblical reference, Vance said, "There was a man in the Scriptures named Jeshurun who waxed fat and kicked. Whenever the office-holders wax fat and kick, the people should wax wrothy and kick them out."[27]

Showing concern for the presidential race, Vance charged that Hayes, the Republican nominee for President, would be no better than Grant. In language vivid in imagery familiar to the country people to whom he was speaking, he said, "It is no use when a setting of eggs had become rotten to put another hen on the same eggs. As things are now, we need a new nest, new eggs, and a new hen."[28]

The final debate was held at Swift Creek on October 21. As usual, Vance regaled his audience with witty denunciations of the opposition party. He emphasized the corruption of the Republicans, and declared it was time to turn them out of office. Using satirical humor, he said:

It was a shrewd thing in the radicals here in North Carolina when they abolished the whipping post before they went stealing. If they had not been sharp enough to do that they would have been the greatest set of striped back and ring-tailed rascals ever seen.[29]

The most significant thing about this last debate was the cordiality of each candidate toward the other. Vance commended the honorable conduct of his opponent, and expressed the hope that whatever the outcome of their forensic duel, it would serve to promote the honor, the happiness, and the prosperity of North Carolina. Judge Settle reciprocated by saying that North Carolina was to be congratulated on the fact that their campaign of fifty-seven days had left no wound that rankled in the heart of either candidate. The two candidates shook hands as they parted, and Vance humorously remarked, "I'm sorry to leave you, old fellow. You've been pretty fair with me while we've been together, but I don't know how it will be when you get off by yourself. I reckon you'll have to swear me in as governor next January."[30]

The debates raised political activities from a degenerate status to a higher plane. It was a hopeful sign that an entire campaign could be conducted without either candidate becoming embittered. The candidates departed as friends.

A typical Democratic rally was held at Kinston on October 23. Vance and his party arrived at the beautiful rural village at eight o'clock in the morning and found a host of people waiting to greet them at the depot. The Greenville cornet band was on hand to play for the festive occasion. When Vance left the train, he found the crowd had formed two parallel lines, ten deep on each side, with each line facing the other. Absolute silence was maintained until the candidate had walked to the end of the line. Then three deafening cheers rent the air. With a horseman bearing a large United States flag leading the way, Vance's carriage was escorted through the main streets of the town by a cavalcade of mounted men, followed by a long procession of people in vehicles and on foot. The porches and windows were filled with ladies waving their handkerchiefs in welcome.

A speaker's stand draped in white, festooned with cedar, ivy, and holly, and interspersed here and there with flowers, had been erected at the south end of the Lenoir County courthouse. A banner at one end of the platform bore the motto, "Vance, the people's choice." Opposite this was a large American flag. At the rear of the platform was a beautifully decorated band wagon. In front of the stand were three thousand people eager to hear what their candidate had to say.[31]

Vance had enjoyed the series of debates and his opening statement suggests that he regretted his opponent was not still with him. He said that in the absence of his competitor he was like a blacksmith beating an anvil without any iron. In his speech he used facts and figures similar to those he had used in the debates, and advanced the basic proposition that a change in the administrations of the national and state government must be made.

Vance pictured the Republican party as being corrupt to the core. He accused it of giving the lie to its own professions, as exemplified by the Emancipation Proclamation which had been issued by Lincoln after Congress declared it had no intention of interfering with slavery. Vance also considered it evil for the Republican party to support the congressional Reconstruction plan, which, he said, resulted in dissolving the Union which they had fought four years to maintain. Vance based this attack on his belief that the Congressional plan provided by the Reconstruction Acts of March 2 and 23, 1867, dissolved the Union by refusing to readmit southern states to the Union until they had met the following requirements: (1) A state had to ratify establishing Negro suffrage; (2) the Fourteenth Amendment to the federal Constitution must be ratified; (3) the state government must be approved by Congress.

Speaking of the treatment received from Congress when the South was admitted, Vance said, "They wanted us to come back, if we came at all, as radicals. They wanted us to play the part of the prodigal son, but when we got home, we were marched around the chimney of the great house right slam into the kitchen."[32]

Vance presented his most convincing appeal toward the end of the speech. In this appeal, he explained to the people that corruption and extravagant expenditures had wasted their money. Convinced that excessive spending showed a weakness in a government, he generalized, "The best government in the world is that which is cheapest."[33]

Declaring that the only reply of Radicals to his charges of corruption and malfeasance was "War! War! War!" he asked, "Is it any reason that you should support thieves because I and my friends are war men?"[34] An internal summary of his theme was then presented in this admonition:

A change may help, but cannot hurt us. If the men the Democrats put in power go back on you, turn them out. Keep turning out and turning out until you get honest men in office.[35]

The election was a sweeping victory for the Democrats. Vance won by a majority of more than thirteen thousand votes, and except for one congressman, every state and national officer selected was a Democrat. Reconstruction had ended, and, says Conner, the administration of the government passed into the hands of the party which represented the intelligence, the property, and the patriotism of North Carolina.[36]

It is impossible to determine to what extent Vance was responsible for the end of Radical rule, but it is safe to conclude that no political speaker in North Carolina had greater power over an audience.

Elaborate plans were made for Vance's inauguration. In spite of a blizzard, a large crowd gathered on January 1 to see the curtain fall "upon the last scene of the last act of the great Reconstruction drama."[37] After taking the oath of office, Vance delivered his third inaugural address as governor of the state of North Carolina.

He began his speech with this timely observation: "There is retribution in history. For all the wrongs and inequalities of individual and national life there is compensation, provided we do but patiently await its coming."[38] The first part of the speech was a review of the argument he had advanced throughout the campaign regarding the fallacy of Reconstruction legislation.

Refraining from his usual humor, he spoke with a degree of reserve and dignity appropriate to the occasion. He scathingly denounced, however, the baser elements of the Radical party in these words:

North Carolina was placed in the hands of the designing and ignorant of our people, organized and led by unscrupulous and disreputable adventurers from the slums of Northern politics; a base and comorant tribe of reptiles which seem to spring like fungi from the rottenness and corruption of revolutionary times.[39]

Although Vance's inaugural address was merely a summary of his campaign speeches, it satisfied the Democrats.

If nothing was said in the inaugural to please the Negroes, their apprehensions were relieved by Vance's message to the General Assembly shortly after the inauguration. In keeping with his efforts to restore an orderly and progressive state government, he advocated an effective school system for the Negroes. He urged the members of the legislature to live up to their pledges and make no discrimination in the matter of public education; but to deal justly and equitably with all school children of the state.[40]

With Vance formally seated as governor, there was rejoicing from "Murphy to Manteo." By his election, "the state had been redeemed, home rule had been restored, and white supremacy had been achieved."[41]

CHAPTER VIII

THIRD TERM GUBERNATORIAL SPEAKING

Vance's earlier terms as governor had been dated from the war years when his chief responsibilities were feeding and clothing the soldiers and keeping able-bodied men in the service of the Confederacy. Although he had successfully fulfilled his duties as a war governor, the people wondered whether he could meet the crises of peace as well. The work before him consisted of restoring the state's depleted economy, and cleansing its corrupt government.

Vance advocated an educated citizenry.[1] Reconstruction had impressed upon him the dangers of government by the ignorant masses. Consequently, he was genuinely concerned with education during his third term.

According to C. H. Mebane, Superintendent of Public Instruction in North Carolina in 1900, ". . . the greatest service that Vance ever rendered the educational interest of North Carolina was when he took a bold stand in 1877 to provide training for teachers." Mebane referred to the governor's message to the General Assembly in which Vance said: "It is impossible for the blind to lead the blind." In the same speech, he also strongly advocated training for Negroes. "A school of similar character as that proposed for training white teachers," he said, "should be established for the education of colored teachers, the want of which is more deeply felt by the black race even than the white."[2]

His first speaking appearance after his inauguration was before the colored Emancipation Society, which met in Metropolitan Hall in Raleigh on January 2, 1877.[3] Perhaps the colored people invited Vance to speak in order to ascertain his policy toward them. The Negroes, commemorating their own emancipation,

86

could hardly be expected to be favorable toward this man who had opposed their emancipation. Vance was well aware of the antagonism that existed in the audience, and his speech demonstrates effective planning to gain a favorable response. He knew that if he were fair and tactful, he would gain a hearing, if not an acceptance of his ideas. Consequently, he began his speech by assuring the audience that his oath of office bound him to respect their rights as well as the rights of the white people. The right that seemed most important to him was that of education. In fairness to all, he had committed himself to equal efforts for the education of both races.[4]

Demonstrating tact, Vance told his audience that he sympathized fully with their efforts to commemorate the event which made them free men. He declared they would be as ungrateful to forget it as he would be wicked to grudge them the joyous celebration of it.

Having thus established himself as a friend of the Negroes, Vance sought to give them what he considered wise advice. The Negroes were voting in a solid block for the Republicans. Vance believed that they were voting as they were told, rather than acting upon their own initiative. With this in mind, he warned that they would never be free until they voted from individual judgment as free men.

The speech was extemporaneous, if not impromptu, and lasted for only an hour. Vance was interrupted frequently by hearty applause.

On January 2, 1878, Vance addressed another Negro audience. The occasion was the fifteenth anniversary of the Emancipation proclamation. The colored chairman of the meeting, John Leary, in introducing Vance, praised him for the conscientious manner in which he administered the affairs of the state, and for the interest he had shown in Negro education. Vance responded with a briefer and less conciliatory speech than he had delivered at Raleigh a year earlier. Frankly stating that he was not there to celebrate their emancipation, he said:

My friends, I appear in your meeting today simply to acknowledge the respect you have shown me by inviting me as Governor of the state to visit your assemblage. You cannot, of course, expect me to join with you in celebrating this day, the anniversary of that emancipation which I struggled so long to prevent, and which I, in common with almost all the people of my race in the South, consider as an act of unconstitutional violence to one party and as an injury to the other.[5]

In one abrupt assertion, Vance concluded the speech by stating it was his duty to recognize the Negroes as citizens, and he would respect all the rights the laws had invested in them. "This," he said, "I cheerfully do, always have done, and always shall do."[6]

The decade of the 1870's was the beginning of an industrial revolution in North Carolina. Cotton mills and tobacco manufacturing made great advances. But while expansion and prosperity were evident in manufacturing and transportation, agriculture suffered from an economic depression which left the farmers impoverished. The problem of the farmers was national in scope. Agricultural leaders had urged the farmers to unite for the general improvement of rural life. The first farmers' organization, the Patrons of Husbandry — commonly called the Grange — was formed in 1869. It was not until March 3, 1875, however, that this movement spread to North Carolina, when the first Grange was organized at McLeansville in Guilford County.

On May 18, 1878, Vance was invited to speak at a Grange picnic. In this address Vance was flexible in his delivery and frequently used dialect or imitated a faulty speech pattern for the sake of humor. Using a juvenile speech manner, he began the address with a story. He said that he had reached the point in politics that the boy had reached in the sugar barrel story. Continuing the narration, he explained:

After stealing sugar for a long time, the old man having exhausted every means but one to break him concluded to put him in a sugar barrel and bead [*sic*] it up, which he accordingly did. After the boy had remained in the barrel for some time the old man asked him if he had enough sugar, the boy replied, 'No I ain't dot nuff, but I dot down where it don't taste dood.'[7]

So it was with Vance, he had reached that point in politics where it "don't taste dood."

This story represents one of the few times Vance told a story that was unrelated to the main idea of his speech. Indeed, Vance so consistently adhered to the principle of relevance that one wonders if this story was actually present in the speech. Perhaps the newspaper reports, which were often inaccurate, omitted a transition that related the introduction to the body of the address.

Vance did a superb job of placing himself on common ground with his audience. Explaining that although it was not possible for a lawyer and politician to tell farmers a great deal about farming, he did know something about agriculture. It was learned, however, outside the fence and not in the field.

After describing the agricultural advantages of North Carolina, he introduced the theme of the speech with two rhetorical questions. "Why is it," he asked, "we are so far behind?" "Why is it we continue to farm scooter style?" Briefly stating the answer, he said, "The farmers need fertilizing as well as the lands."[8]

In this speech Vance showed his usual care in the arrangement of ideas. He said that there were four duties for the farmer to perform. These were:

1st, Improve your farms; it is a duty you owe to yourself, to posterity, to leave your land better than you found it.
2nd, It is your duty to grow your provisions at home.
3rd, Preserve your forests, for our timber has been used too lavishly.
4th, The promotion of education was a matter of greatest importance to both races.[9]

Evidently presuming that the first three duties were self-explanatory, Vance spent most of his time in amplifying the fourth point. He accused both races of being deficient in education, and charged that some members of each seemed to think they could get along with amazingly little schooling. "In fact," he said, "they haven't got enough to know that they don't know anything."[10]

Although Vance used many forms of humor, he found exaggeration especially effective. Using it to describe the quantity and quality of dogs, he said, "In North Carolina there are two dogs to one sheep, and many of these are so poor they have to lean against the house to bark."[11]

Another opportunity for Vance to expound his philosophy of education came on July 22 of the same year. He addressed the teachers enrolled in the summer session at the newly established normal school of the university. Explaining why he had asked the legislature for an appropriation for training teachers, he said that teachers were "tools," and with dull tools a good day's work could not be done. There were plenty of dull tools in North Carolina. In fact, it was next to impossible to find competent teachers. The records of county examiners showed that most applicants for teaching were deficient in the basic skills of reading, spelling, writing, and arithmetic.

A few days later, on July 27, 1878, Vance more clearly developed his new educational program in an address to fifteen hundred pupils and patrons of the Wilson Collegiate Institute. Boldly stating his theme in the introduction, he asserted that there was a weakness in contemporary education. This weakness he attributed to the fact that too much effort was devoted to an "ornamental education which is eminently useful and proper to a wealthy people to the neglect of the practical kind which is best suited to a poor community."[12]

Vance was probably the first governor of North Carolina to advocate technical or vocational training in preference to the traditional liberal arts education. Only a small percentage of the people concerned themselves with higher education. Those who went to college attended the University of North Carolina or one of the three denominational schools in the state, Davidson, Wake Forest, or Trinity, now Duke University. All of these schools offered a thorough classical education, but showed little or no interest in any other kind of training. The University in particular had defaulted in its opportunity to offer industrial and agricultural education. Soon after North Carolina was readmitted to the Union in 1868, it received as a result of the Morrill Act, better known as the Land Grant Colleges Act, the land script for 270,000 acres of public land, which it sold for $125,000. For several years the university received $7,500 in interest on the original $125,000. This money was designed to provide agricultural and mechanical education. Although the university offered a few courses in these subjects, their offerings were too limited to attract many students.[13]

Vance thought this situation deplorable. The state, he said, was badly in need of skilled workers, but nothing was being done to train them. He declared:

Youths receiving a liberal education in our college curriculums are in excess of those who are receiving a practical education. The market for Latin and Greek scholars is already glutted, whilst the demand for skillfully educated practical men is very great.[14]

During the course of the speech, Vance used illustrations to make his ideas vivid and clear to the heterogeneous group of students and patrons who were in attendance. To clarify his theme, he told the story of the philosopher, who in crossing a stream asked the boatman many questions about the water. When he learned that the boatman knew nothing whatever about it, he held up his hands in horror, exclaiming, "My conscience, what ignorance!" In a little while the water began to pour through a seam in the boat. After attempting to stop it, the boatman asked the philosopher if he could swim. The answer was "No." Then exclaimed the boatman, "My God, what ignorance! I am going to swim ashore and you are going to the bottom."[15] This simple illustration vividly reflected the main idea of the speech — that providing an ornamental education to the exclusion of a practical one might prove disastrous to the state.

Many of Vance's third-term gubernatorial speeches were of inferior quality which may be attributed to the adverse conditions under which he labored. In addition to being heavily burdened with the duties of his office, he also worked under the strain of grief. Within less than a month apart, both his elderly mother and wife died. This double loss was deeply felt by Vance who attributed much of his success to the influence of these women.

Although Vance's grief was strong, it gradually lessened with the passage of time. He lost himself in his work, and his ambition to return to the Senate took a prominent place in his life. As early as June 1878, it was common knowledge that he wanted to replace Senator A. S. Merrimon, whose term would expire at the end of the next session of Congress. Merrimon's friends and supporters became critical of Vance's efforts. One Democrat, strongly expressing himself, said, "Whenever North Carolina commits this political crime, let her hide her face in shame forever."[16] But six months later, the General Assembly elected him by acclamation. A committee of five legislators was appointed to inform Governor Vance of his election. They escorted him to the General Assembly, where he was introduced to the joint session by the speaker of the House.[17]

On January 28, 1879, Vance sent his resignation to the General Assembly, asking to be released as governor in order that he might take his seat in the Senate. On March 4 he entered the Senate, where for the remainder of his life he was destined to labor and speak on behalf of his state and nation.[18]

resigned as governor to become a senator

CHAPTER IX

SENATORIAL SPEAKING

During a period of dullness and apathy in national politics Vance was seated in the Senate of the Forty-sixth Congress on March 18, 1879. Instead of dealing with great issues, congressmen were engaged in petty bickering on partisan and sectional matters. The Republican President, Rutherford B. Hayes, did not initiate legislation because he was certain that it would be defeated by the predominantly Democratic Congress; and the Congress, certain of a presidential veto, initiated very little.

Vance immediately showed an interest in all discussions, and soon engaged in making incidental remarks, many of which were humorous in nature and added a touch of variety to the monotonous congressional sessions. An interesting commentary on his humor appeared in the Philadelphia *Times* shortly after he took office:

Our legislative bodies are humdrum enough to suit a conclave of rueful visaged owls. In our courts there are occasional flashes of the jocular. . . . We have had tragedy enough of late years. We need a revival of the comic. Who is the coming man to answer this great national want by inaugurating a regime of wholesome hearty fun in high places? The era of good feeling can never be brought about by sober companions and concessions.

Zebulon B. Vance is a wag of the first water. His brain secretes jokes as other men's brains do ideas of a merely rationalistic nature. . . . His wit never smacks of the cloister. It is not studied, and elaborate, and odorous of the lamp. The fascination of his fun is in its spontaniety, its originality and the inexhaustible fecundity of the imagination

93

which generates it. His mind is a vast reservoir of humor, fed by perennial springs, ever full and always running over. The readiness of his inventive faculty in this direction is as marvelous as its fertility.

Vance has a great deal of bonhommie, that fine element of popular leadership which attracts men more than what is called personal magnetism does. There is no bitterness about him. His humor is always tempered by good nature. When he arraigns Republicanism, it is as something way off and the present company is courteously excepted. . . .[1]

Typical of Vance at this period is the following:

One Senator, as his argument, cries out rebellion; another cries out secession; another exclaims with alarm that rebel soldiers are here in these Halls; another claims that the North pays a larger part of the direct taxes and nearly all the taxes collected on imports; another sees a goblin in the shape of a Democratic caucus; another holds up his hands in holy horror in contemplating the fact that there is absolutely a Democratic majority in both branches of Congress; and yet another sees ruin in a solid South and last but not least, one Senator exclaims in the famine of argument, 'Jefferson Davis;' and that is the contribution that he furnishes to the literature of his country.[2]

Responding to Republican attacks on the Solid South, he asked, "Who made the South solid?" He followed this rhetorical question with the answer — the Republican party was responsible. Reasoning that the acts of the Republican party during Reconstruction were the direct cause, he explained:

At the beginning of the late war almost the entire Whig party of the South, with a large and influential portion of the Democratic, were in favor of the Union and deprecated with their whole souls the attempts at its destruction, but through love of their native states and sympathy with their kindred and neighbors they were drawn into the support of the war. What became of them after the war? Their wisdom in opposing it was justified by the ruinous results; their patriotism and courage were highly appreciated, and when peace came this class was in high favor at the South, while the secessionists as the original advocates of a disastrous policy were down in public estimation.

If the gentlemen of the North had then come forward with liberal terms and taken these men by the hand, you would have perpetuated your power in this government for a generation, provided you had listened to the views of those men and respected their policy on questions touching their section. But you pursued the very opposite course. A course which compelled almost every decent, intelligent man of Anglo-Saxon prejudices and traditions to take a firm and determined stand against you. . . .[3]

Vance replied to the senators who had expressed fear of a Congress controlled by the Democrats by asking if this constituted a real danger to the best interests of the country. In his opinion it did not, because the country owed its chief glory and development to the Democratic party. Without the Democratic party, he believed, the United States would be a feeble and second-class nation.

Specifically, Vance credited the Democratic party with extending the boundaries of the Republic from the Mississippi River to the Pacific Ocean. "As I now remember," he said, "not a single foot of land has been added to the empire by the Republican party, except Alaska." Vance, agreeing with those who thought of the purchase of Alaska as "Seward's folly," considered the vast territory acquired from the Russians as "a broad stretch of icy waste, a land where frozen earth contends with frozen water, inhabited by seals and savages, in a climate which I have heard described as nine months of winter and three months of damnation cold weather."[4]

The novel arrangement of the speech heightened its effect. To illustrate absurdity of his opponents' arguments Vance framed them into the form of mathematical propositions. A single example of this will show the style of his attack:

Proposition first: Theorem — The troops of the United States are two thousand miles away on the frontier and could not be used to control elections if they wanted. — Senator from Maine. The troops could not be used if they were here, as the law forbids it. I promise not to use them. — The president. Corrollary first. — The necessity for troops at the polls to secure fair elections is in proportion to the squares of the distance of their present location, i.e. the greater the distance, the greater the necessity.
Corrollary second. — The necessity for the presence of troops at the polls is also in proportion to the legal inability to use them if they

were present, and if the President is determined not to use them at all to control elections, then the necessity becomes absolute.

Corrollary third. — The revolutionary and dangerous character of a law consists in the fact that it is useless there being already in existence laws sufficient to effect the purpose.

Scholium. — In the above it is assumed axiomatically that the terms 'liberty' and 'purity of elections' are synonymous with the term 'Republican party.'[5]

In this speech Vance was answering not only Senator Blaine, but also the arguments which many Republican senators had presented. One Senator had gravely declared that the election laws should not be repealed because the bulk of the army was in the West while only about 30,000 soldiers were in North Carolina, which was too small a number to cause any fear. Answering this argument, Vance used a series of parallelisms, which were clearly and vividly stated in figurative language, making the fears of the South analogous to fears which the audience had experienced or read about. He said:

... We fear them as the Hollander fears the first small leak in the dikes which bear back the waves of the ocean from deluging the meadows of his homestead; we fear them as the physician fears the first speck of gangrene in the system of his patient; we fear them as the sailor fears the piling up of the storm clouds upon the horizon, knowing that their deceptive beauty covers the fierce desolation of the tempest; we fear them as the shepherd of the mountain fears for his lambs at even with the flitting of a shadow athwart his path, for he knows it to be the shadow of the eagle, the remorseless tyrant of the air; we fear them as Charlemagne feared the rude wooden ships of the Norse Vikings on their first appearance in the seas of his empire; we fear them as all patriotic Romans feared the crossing of the Rubicon by Caesar, the passage of which with arms in his hands marked him as the enemy of Roman liberty.[6]

The speech was significant mainly because it was Vance's first speech in the Senate, and it provided a preview of the style his senatorial speaking was to assume. He read the speech from manuscript — a revolutionary change from his earlier extemporaneous style — but he maintained his usual forceful delivery. During its course, the audience laughed heartily at his occasional ancedotes and humorous remarks.

As Vance continued his senatorial speaking during the remainder of his life, he was chiefly concerned with three objects — silver, civil service, and tariff. His interest in these subjects inspired his major speeches, which led to his becoming a popular speaker.[7] Yet he did not spend all of his time on the floor of the Senate. Many hours and days were given over to committee meetings, and to making political addresses in behalf of various Democratic candidates.[8]

On July 2, 1881, President Garfield was shot by a disappointed office seeker, and Vice-President Arthur was elevated to the presidency. Arthur was a New York machine politician who had been controlled by the lordly Conkling. There was little in Arthur's record to presage a good administration. Unexpectedly, however, he demonstrated genuine independence,[9] and in his message to the first session of the Forty-seventh Congress on December 5, 1881, came out strongly in favor of civil service and tariff reform.[10]

These tariff reform bills soon claimed Vance's attention. In the closing days of the first session of the Forty-seventh Congress, on July 26, 1882, he was prompted to speak on the Internal Revenue bill, which had already been passed by the House of Representatives. Vance favored tariff relief, but not the spurious type proposed by the Republican bill. He wanted the relief to benefit the masses rather than the monied interests. Consequently, he made a witty, interesting speech asking for a tariff revision that would reduce taxes on essential commodities. The speech was embellished with his usual supply of well-told stories, along with an abundance of ridicule concerning the abolition of taxes on banks, perfumery, matches, and patent medicine.[11]

Expressing his basic philosophy on taxation, Vance said he was opposed to placing a tax on any item which was generally used by all people.[12] He continued to advocate this philosophy in future tariff debates and wherever the opportunity arose.[13]

The placid administration of Arthur ended in the most exciting presidential campaign since the Civil War. The Republicans nominated Blaine; the Democrats, Grover Cleveland. Blaine was unacceptable to many honest Republicans, and they switched to the support of Cleveland. After a bitter campaign, Cleveland won the election.

The first great issue on which Vance and Cleveland differed was the silver question. Vance believed in bimetallism, while Cleveland recommended in his message to Congress, December 8, 1885, that the Silver Coinage Act be suspended.[14] This issue placed the farmers of the West and South in conflict with the industrialists of the East. The farmers had long favored inflation of the currency as a method of attaining prosperity. "Inflate the currency," said one senator, "and you raise the price of my steers."[15] While supporting a bill offered by Senator James B. Beck of Kentucky, Vance made a speech on behalf of the doctrine of bimetallism. The bill proposed that the Secretary of the Treasury should meet all payments of interest with gold and silver coin.[16]

Another question that arose early in Cleveland's administration was that of patronage. Democrats, deprived of the spoils of office for twenty-five years, demanded a clean sweep of office-holders. The Mugwumps, the label attached to the Republicans who had supported Cleveland, insisted that there be no sweep at all. But a cry of protest arose when the President failed to award spoils to the regular workers of the Democratic party. Vance, differing with the President on this issue, introduced a bill to repeal the Civil Service law in order to make public offices spoils of partisan victory.[17]

Vance showed considerable temerity in presenting this bill, because he knew that it had little chance of passing. He said that he was in earnest and would speak in support of the bill, but he did not expect many votes, because those in favor of the bill did not have the courage of their convictions. Commenting on Vance's anticipated speech, the *New York Times* made political capital of his tendency to use humor which was at times risque. The paper said:

Vance will doubtless have a day when he will address the senate. When that happens, the next number of the *Record* will be interesting reading. It will contain much vulgarity and much that a Senator of this generation ought to be ashamed of, but it will not be dull.[19]

The prediction by the *Times* that Vance would address the Senate on the proposed bill came true, but the expected vulgarity did not materialize. On January 12, 1886, Vance delivered the longest speech he had given since becoming a senator. It was replete with arguments, but contained little that was humorous. Although the *Times* was inaccurate in part of its prediction, it may have had grounds for expecting Vance to use poor taste in the selection of anecdotes for the speech. He was evidently in the habit of telling such stories, but they were deleted before the speeches were published. The *Chicago Daily News* declared, "His chief fame in Washington rests upon his success as a relator of tales which would hardly bear repetition in polite society."[20]

Although there was possibly some truth in the indictment by the *News,* it was not completely true. Vance was often serious in his speeches before the Senate. Typical of his more serious efforts was the speech on Civil Service which he delivered on March 31, 1886. Deviating from his usual practice, he lost the spontaneity and individuality that made him an effective speaker, and became simply one of the seventy-six senators, each of whom could read from manuscript as well as Vance. Observers considered him at his best in his senatorial speaking "when Vance was Vance."[21]

Vance's chief objection to the Civil Service law, which his proposed bill sought to repeal, was that it defeated the will of the people as expressed at popular elections, and impaired the vigor and efficiency of political parties in the country. "I believe," he said, "most earnestly that parties are indispensable to the existence of liberty, and that a government by the party is the only way in which there can be government by the people." To support this belief he quoted from the following men of letters and political science:

Party, says Edmund Burke, is a body of men united for promoting by their joint endeavors the national interest upon some particular principle in which they are all agreed. Men thinking freely will in particular instances think differently. But still as the greater part of the measures which arise in the course of public business are related to, or dependent on, some great leading, general principles in government, a man must be peculiarly unfortunate in the choice of his political company if he does not agree with them at least nine times in ten, and this is all that ever was required for a character of the greatest uniformity and steadiness in connection. How men can proceed without connection at all is to me incomprehensible.

Lord John Russell, in his essay on the English Government and Constitution, says:

Now of the two ways of procuring adherents — the attachment of interest and that of party — party is by far the best. Many a man I fear would abandon his opinions and fall off from his principles for the sake of office who will yet not desert a party to which he is engaged by passion and affection as well as by reason. . . .

Says Mr. Madison: No free country has ever been without parties, which are a natural offspring of freedom.

Says Francis Lieber in his *Political Ethics:* I believe there never existed a free country actively developing within its bosom constitutional law and feeling deeply interested in the great problems of right and public justice in which there were not also parties. . . .

Says Horace Walpole: I have a maxim — that the extinction of party is the origin of faction.[22]

Vance's use of testimony to prove the value of political parties was adequate. The authorities were reliable, and were recognized as able and competent men. The weakness in his argument lay in the lack of a cause and effect relationship between the merit system and the destruction of political parties. He offered no evidence to prove this point, while he spent much time on the irrelevent point that political parties are advantageous.

Vance organized the speech against the Civil Service law under two main points. First, he said the law was an attack upon the rightful prerogative of the President; second, it defeated the will of the people as expressed at popular elections, and consequently impaired the effectiveness of political parties.

Although the speech showed less sarcastic invective than he customarily used, his tirade against those who professed to be political Independents contained a noticeable degree of it. He said that he could find among the Independents "only mock philosophers, sentimental women, and effeminate men, whose principles were sickly sentimental, Sunday School 'Goody Two-Shoes' kind."[23]

Nowhere in the speech was there evidence of conciliation or compromise. In the conclusion, which reflected the same defiant spirit found in the introduction and body, he declared:

Between those who call me a spoilsman and myself there is perhaps only a difference of definition. They believe that reform consists in a Democratic administration operated by Republican agents; I do not. They believe in keeping Republicans in office by the law after the people have declared they shall go out; I do not. They believe in ignoring the people of officials; I do not. They believe there can be no sincere reforms unless Republicans are the chief beneficiaries thereof; I do not. And lastly, I believe that as good material for all civil officials is to be found in the Democratic party as in any other, and that it is the right and duty of a Democratic administration to select the material and none other as elements of reform; they do not.

Let me warn men against those who assume to be above the homely virtues and common frailties of our race, and who affect to inhabit the untrodden altitudes of a world different from the one where our creator has placed us, and deny being of the earth, earthy. A man too good in politics or religion is quite reprehensible as one too bad, and I am quite sure he is a greater nuisance. For the most part they are men who have failed in securing the objects of their own ambition, and may be described either as political old maids whose blood has turned to vinegar by a failure to secure lovers before their unappreciated charms had fled, or as grass widows of politics without the aid of politicians who believe that the most successful way to operate mechanics is to work without implements.[24]

This was the only speech Vance made in the Senate on Civil Service reform; however, as the principal speaker for the Fourth of July celebration in 1886 at Tammany Hall he again attacked the Civil Service reform law.

In spite of words of encouragement and of Vance's popularity as a speaker, there were not sufficient votes for passage of the bill. It was tabled on June 18, 1886.[25]

The differences between Vance and the President on the two major issues of silver and civil service produced a breach which caused Vance openly to avow his opposition to Cleveland. In 1887 Vance stated emphatically that he was not a Cleveland man. "The President," he said, "is not of my school of Democracy. We differ as widely on several national issues as is possible for two persons belonging to the same political party."[26]

On October 8, 1888, the tariff debate opened formally over a bill to reduce taxation and simplify the laws in relation to the collection of revenue. A battle for supremacy was staged between the Republican advocates of high tariff and the Democratic champions of tariff reduction. Vance opened the debate for the proponents of low tariff. Expressing a purely partisan point of view, which had the support of the Democrats in Congress, he said:

Common sense and common honesty suggested that it [tariff reduction] should be made upon those things where the inequalities were greatest and where the relief to the people would be greatest, to wit, upon the necessaries in greatest use by the most people.[27]

Vance's basic beliefs on the tariff were derived from his associations with an agricultural people. He believed that the increased costs of the bare necessities of life resulting from high tariff worked an undue hardship on the farmers. Observation of the people of his state provided him with insight sufficient for a strong attack upon the Finance Committee's claim that the substitute bill would benefit the people and carry confidence and comfort into American homes. He said:

Into some of them it will carry this confidence and comfort, no doubt. The committee did not venture to say all American homes. Into the home of Mr. Carnegie, Mr. Havemeyer, Mr. Ammidown, and every great manufacturer and every member of a trust it will no doubt be warmly received. These homes are found in the palaces.

But in the homes of the cabin and the cottage, in the farmsteads amid the blooming orchards, in the humble habitation of the widow and the orphan the continued tax on their salt, their children's books and slate pencils, their tin-cups and water-pails, the increased tax upon their woolen and cotton clothing, their table cutlery, plates, cups and saucers, their blankets and wool hats will carry neither confidence nor comfort. It will rather make the thoughtful among them wonder why in the name of a merciful Creator a free Christian government will thus lade them with this weight of taxation and scrimp their narrow means still more for the benefit of those who are already rich.[28]

The points Vance made were supported by the use of statistics. Relying upon data gathered from the census reports, he showed that since the war the agricultural classes had not enjoyed as much prosperity as the rest of the nation:

Nowhere has the decay of agriculture been more marked and lamentable than in several of the New England states where manufactures most abound. The statistics of these states completely refute the idea that manufactures furnish a home market which enriches the farmer...whilst cities and towns of New England have grown and become wealthy by the protective policy; it has been at the expense and decay of the country at large.

The tendency of the population in all our Northern country to rush to the cities is one of the social evils of the times, which legislation should do nothing to encourage if it can do nothing to check. This tendency in New England is particularly noticeable. Massachusetts, the richest and most populous of those states, is undergoing this process of popular congestion — this rushing of the social blood to the head — at a galloping rate.

He provided statistical proof for his remarks and showed that income from agriculture had declined, and that population was surging to the cities of the Northeast. There were few people left on the farms in these states; the majority had forsaken farming for work in industry. He agreed that the protective tariff protected

the capitalist engaged in manufacturing, but argued that it did
so at the expense of destroying agriculture. This he opposed. "Of
all the people in America who support the protective policy," he
said, "the last to give it aid, should be the masses . . . especially
the agricultural population."[29]

The dullness of the statistics was brightened by Vance's use
of vivid illustrations which explained the inference to be drawn
from them. The following pictorial view of New England farm
land is typical:

Connecticut and Massachusetts, formerly covered with fruitful meadows and grain fields, are now unprofitably gay with sumac and odorous fern. The once cultivated land is occupied by brush and brake
and the woodman plies his ax where seventy-five years ago were heard
the ring of the scythe and rustle of the sickle.[30]

He accused the Finance Committee of having made the changes
in the classification of duty-free items to satisfy the manufacturing
interests, rather than to relieve the people of a tax burden. Reducing to an absurdity the Republicans' arguments that the substitute bill would benefit all the people, he spoke sarcastically:

Their free-list is a fair indication of their regard for those neglected
sixty millions. Acorns, baryta, beeswax, braids, bristles, chickory, culm,
coal-tar, curling-stone handles, Zanta for smoking, rags, rape-seed,
sponges and sand show their respect for the comfort of the millions.
Books printed in foreign tongues, which little children can not read,
are also free. This, with free opium, is intended doubtless as a bonus
to that peculiar American labor for which protection is invoked. With
the exception of jute and jute-butts and textile grasses and cheap
adulterated molasses there is little upon it worth anything to anybody
except the manufacturers. Compare it with the blessings conferred on
the poor by the free-list of the House bill-free wool, lumber, salt, cotton ties and in plate.[31]

Vance kept a good balance between logical proofs and emotional
appeals throughout this speech. His emotional appeals were short,
and were used as adjuncts to reason rather than as substitutes. He

appealed to fair play and pity as he answered the senators who said they intended to reserve the home market for their own people if it meant building a Chinese wall around the United States to exclude all foreign products:

Meantime the consumer, finding prices at home put up on him, is not permitted to buy abroad by the tariff, must pay whatever prices are demanded of him for his supplies, and must sell his own products in glutted markets at home. Thus is the American farmer situated by the beauties of this home-market theory which he is invited to support. Before him stands that high Chinese wall which excludes him from the outer world; behind him stand the trusts armed with corporate powers to inflict penalties upon any treacherous member who shall offer to sell him anything below the regulation price!! The fact that any of them still hold the title deeds to their farms, still have decent clothing for their families and sufficient implements for their business, designate them as being special favorites of the gods, who have stamped them with unmistakable marks of immortality.[32]

Basically the speech was partisan rather than sectional. The Democrats of the entire country favored a reduction in the tariff, and Vance came to the defense of Cleveland against the attacks of the Republicans. The Republicans blamed the President for the accumulation of a surplus which made a tariff reduction feasible.

The tariff was one of the few issues on which Vance and Cleveland agreed, and Vance answered the Republicans' charge by saying: "It is true he could [have spent the surplus], and so he could have squandered it as countless millions have been squandered under the administrations of his predecessors, but he did not."[33]

A month after Vance's participation in the tariff debate, the election of 1888 was held. Benjamin Harrison was the Republican opponent of President Cleveland. Although differing with Cleveland on many issues, Vance made many speeches in various parts of the country on behalf of his candidacy.[34] On November 7, 1888, Cleveland, who won the most popular votes, lost to Harrison who received the most electoral votes. In this election the Republicans also gained control of both houses of Congress.

During the second session of the Fiftieth Congress, no significant legislation was passed. The lame-duck senate killed time until the Republicans would take over the reins of government.[35] Vance made no significant speeches in this session, although he continued to participate in all tariff debates.[36]

Vance's political career reached its climax in 1890. Both in and out of the senate he spoke more than he had ever spoken before.[37] He was interested in most of the issues surrounding the passage of the Sherman Anti-Trust Act, the Sherman Silver Purchase Bill, and the McKinley Tariff Bill.[38] In addition to speaking on these bills in the senate, he found it necessary to speak in his home state in an effort to retain a favorable majority in the legislature.

During 1890 he had worked so hard in the committee room, and had made so many speeches that toward the end of the year, Vance suffered a breakdown. One side of his face became paralyzed. His sight was affected, and one of his eyes had to be removed in order to save the other one and prevent total blindness. After the operation, in the hope of recovering his health, he visited England, France, Scotland, Ireland, and Italy.[39] This trip abroad evidently did him little good, for his health continued to decline after his return home.

Even if Vance's health had permitted his active participation in the Fifty-second Congress, he probably could have accomplished little. The House was Democratic; the Senate was Republican. The political revolution continued in the presidential election of 1892 when Cleveland defeated Harrison, the Republican incumbent.[40] During this campaign, Vance was advised by friends to conserve his health;[41] consequently, his only public utterance was a speech in support of Cleveland which was published in North Carolina newspapers.[42]

After spending some time recuperating at Wilmington and at Gombroon, his summer home in the mountains,[43] Vance was able to return to Washington in June of 1893.[44] At the opening of the special session, he found himself again opposing Cleveland on the silver issue — specifically, the repeal of the Sherman Silver Purchase Act of 1890.

On September 2, 1893, Vance made his last speech in the senate. The House bill to repeal part of the Sherman Silver Purchase Act was to come before the senate at two o'clock, but Senator Daniel W. Voorhees of Indiana moved to consider the bill in the morning since Vance was then present to speak. Taking as his theme the economic principle that prices were high when money was plentiful and low when money was scarce, Vance spoke for an hour and forty minutes.

Weakened by illness, Vance had lost much of his old-time fire, and was difficult to hear. He still pleased his audience, however, with his usual flow of Scriptural and classical quotations. The *New York Times* was perhaps correct in judging the speech as unimportant, because Vance advanced nothing new.

Using inductive argument, he attempted to prove that the financial crisis was not the result of an oversupply of silver, as Cleveland contended, but rather the result of the destruction of silver. He gave the names of specific countries, starting with England, that had demonetized their silver, and said that demonetization had in each case resulted in lower prices for products.

Vance pointed out inconsistencies in the argument of a House member who said that the repeal of the Sherman Act would save silver rather than destroy it. He stated:

They declare they love silver money, bimetallism; therefore they slay it. They want both metals; therefore they abolish one. They want gold and silver coined on terms of equality, according to their platform, and so they stop coining silver in order to better restore it.

They want to maintain the parity between the two metals, therefore they cut the only cord that holds silver up and permit it to drop out of sight, displaying thereby the same wisdom which was displayed by the Irishman who was going down the shaft of a mine in a bucket and got scared. He shouted: 'Haul me up, boys, haul me up! If you don't haul me up, may the devil fly away with me if I don't cut the rope!'

Truly they must love silver much, since they chastise it much. We will suppose a man is ill and on his bed — the kind physician doctoring him in vain — he slowly sinks, his pulse is low and feeble. Finally a bolder physician comes in who practices on the heroic theory, and he

says to others, "You are all wrong and wasting time in trying to restore
this man by nursing and stimulating him; he will never get up that
way in the world. Let us try a new play; let us cut his throat and take
a new start; we can adopt other remedies for his restoration to life
after that.[45]

With prophetic wisdom Vance predicted that there would be
no legislation favorable to silver if it were not passed at the time of
the repeal of the Sherman Act. He felt strongly that President
Cleveland and the Democratic supporters of the bill were failing
to abide by the Democratic platform adopted at the Chicago convention, and, therefore, were unfaithful to the trust of the people:

Mr. President, we know that it would not become a law; and it
strikes me, sir, that to permit the passage of this bill without attaching
some other legislation could not be secured independently and by
itself — that we consciously surrender and turn our backs upon all the
pledges we have made to the people. It strikes me, sir, that if we do
this we must do it with our eyes open to the consequences; we must
do it knowing that we are subjecting ourselves to the serious accusa-
tions of our constituents.[46]

Seemingly aware that this would be his last speech, he expressed
his deep sincerity in this plea:

... I say that if we pass this bill now unconditionally, that this great
party will then cease to be the peoples' and become the subservient
tool of combined capital. . . .
I speak plainly upon this subject Mr. President, because I feel
deeply, I am too old — I have been too long in public life. I have been
too greatly trusted and honored by the people of my state — to make
myself a party now to anything which appears to me may be construed
as a want of faith to public professions.[47]

Vance concluded the speech with a strong emotional appeal.
The peroration of his last public utterance was in these words:

Surely the fountains of the great deep of humanity are broken up and
the hearts of men are stirred within them as they have never been

stirred before since the Civil War. The great fight is on; the power of money and its allies throughout the world have entered into this conspiracy to perpetrate "the greatest crime of this or any other age," to overthrow one half of the world's money, and thereby double their own wealth by enhancing in value of the other half, which is in their hands. The money changers are polluting the temple of our liberties. "To your tents, O Israel!"[48]

With this exhortation the Tarheel spokesman ended his speaking career. His stalwart frame had become weak and feeble, and his voice had lost its peculiar charm and power. Sad was the contrast of the Vance speaking on the Sherman Act repeal, and Vance making his first speech on the silver issue in 1886. At the time of the earlier speech he was a handsome man weighing 250 pounds and standing six feet tall. How changed in appearance as he delivered his last speech. Blind in one eye, his body stooped, he looked like a feeble old man.

But in spite of his physical feebleness, Vance put forth a strong effort in his final plea for the common man. He had not proceeded far into the speech before he appeared to be physically renewed as he mustered all his strength to appeal for the legislation that he believed vital to the best interest of his people. After he had finished speaking, his weariness was again evident. When Congressman William T. Crawford of North Carolina congratulated him saying, "Governor, you seem to be yourself again," he replied, "By no means; I am thoroughly exhausted." The Tarheel Spokesman then walked from the Senate chamber through doors that closed behind him forever.[49]

CHAPTER X

OCCASIONAL SPEAKING

The occasional speech is as old as public address itself; however, the ancient rhetoricians called it by other names and limited its scope. To Aristotle such speeches were epideictic, and had as their object praise or blame.[1] Among the ancients these speeches were limited chiefly to commemorative addresses upon the gods, men, cities, places, or public works. Today, the scope of occasional speeches has expanded until it includes speeches of courtesy, after-dinner speeches, and the popular lecture.[2] Men of oratorical prominence often find themselves engaged in such speaking, and Vance did a great amount of it during his lifetime. After the war, when necessity required him to make a living by public speaking, he became popular as an occasional speaker and continued in demand for the remainder of his life.

Due to the large number of occasional speeches delivered by Vance, only the more significant ones can be considered in this study. Attention will first be directed toward his commencement addresses, which comprised a considerable part of his speaking.

A typical commencement address was the speech delivered before the graduating class and the literary societies of Wake Forest College on June 26, 1872. Although this address is one of Vance's lesser known speeches, it is representative of his commencement speaking. For this reason, along with the high quality of the speech, it deserves recognition and study.

Ideal commencement subjects are difficult to find, and consequently, such addresses are usually stereotyped. Whether Vance's choice for the Wake Forest address was ideal or not, the address itself was not stereotyped. He showed ingenuity in choosing a theme that was appropriate to audience, occasion, and speaker. His theme was politics, "not politics in its ordinary partisan sense but politics embracing [the] vital and elemental principles of government."[3] He thought this subject was appropriate for the audience, because it was practical and important for college graduates to know something about politics as they began their careers as citizens in a free country. The subject was appropriate for the occasion because it offered guidance to the graduates — a recognized requirement of a commencement address.

In the exordium, Vance established himself as an authority in the field of politics and assured the audience of the appropriateness of the subject:

In accordance with what is appropriate, I will speak to you today about things with which I am most familiar; and which are at the same time most practical and important. I shall speak to you of politics; not of partisan war-cries and stump appeals, but of those vital and elemental principles of Government of which it behooves us to think and talk much, and by which we live and move and have our social being.[4]

The content of the address was a work of art as a commencement address should be. It was generally designed to please the audience and appeal to their esthetic tastes. In the speech Vance was careful to avoid making antagonizing statements, but through the subtle use of suggestion he sought to inspire the audience toward ethical conduct in political affairs. In a plain style, he vividly described the cycle from birth to death of a free born civilization:

There is the birth, — the child-nation brought forth in the manger of poverty, and feebly existing amid the blows and neglects of the world. It is nourished by the self-denial, the bravery, the suffering, the virtue and simplicity of a primitive era. The individual freedom of its members is the basis of that national liberty which pervades all its institutions.... Then comes pride and the accumulation of the means to gratify that insatiate passion — Wealth.
By this time the child has become a giant; simplicity is forgotten;

poverty is despised; and the freedom which was so inestimable in the beginning has become a thing of small consideration.

Then comes luxury, effeminancy, corruption, cruelty, slavery, decay, bloody death and night.[5]

The speech was pleasing to the audience in that it sought to stimulate thought rather than to force belief upon them. Vance clearly stated that the speech was not a politician's bombast to lead the audience into forming political opinions:

In the hope, not of giving you any new information of great value, but of directing your serious attention to these known matters of most vital import to us and our children, I propose to go over the ground briefly with you today; point out our dangers and suggest the remedies.

I desire, earnestly, to do this in a philosophical spirit, and to warn you from, instead of lead you into, the great error of forming your political opinions and principles from the rant of the hustings and flaunting lies of party trickery.[6]

The artistic nature of the speech was again demonstrated in Vance's choice of language and ideas. To support the generalization that liberty is of poor and lowly birth, and languishes by too much contact with the rich, he used a historical fact couched in pleasing poetic language. He said that Roman liberty was born "among the shepherds of the Latian hills, . . . dwelling in the open fields and within mud hovels of its devotees. It perished miserably in the palaces of the Caesars."[7]

Vance used language that was sufficiently exalted for the ideas presented, but it was not ostentatious. He chose concrete, vivid words, rather than abstract, stilted, or high sounding ones. The exalted concrete style of his elaboration on the belief that learning and intelligence are not guarantees of liberty may be observed in the following passage:

Nor can we rely upon the spread of learning and intelligence, to preserve the free institutions of our fathers in all their vigor and purity. History is a wonderful destroyer of theories, and this fond one of ours is likely to be overthrown by facts. If intelligence and virtue

were synonymous, our confidence in it would be justified. But educated
men are no more always virtuous than ignorance is always wicked. And
I believe that educated bad men, in all ages, have done more hurt to
the world than all the ignorance that has ever existed. How many
nations have lost their liberties through the wickedness of the learned?
The brightest age of Athenian eloquence, philosophy and art, made
the least resistance to corruption. The noblest orator, and the greatest
poet of the Augustan age of Roman letters vied in the glorification of
despotism and venality. The polite reign of Charles II rotted England
to the core, and laid her liberties so low that only revolution and a
change of dynasty could revive them. When the "Goddess of Reason"
was enthroned in France, the Goddess of Liberty fled instinctively as
from the face of a favored rival; and a despotism — the worst that
ever cursed any land — a despotism — of the mob — gaunt and bloody
— loomed up at the side of his throne of "Intelligence," — its dark and
overshadowing, and most proper Aegis.[8]

Another artistic device which Vance used in the address, was the
elevation of language by the skillful use of figures of speech. He
spoke of the "noblest valley that ever spread its bosom to the sun,"
"the strong arm of the government," "digging ores from the bosom
of the country," and "building railroads upon its face."[9]

The speech took on added beauty through Vance's rhythmical
prose style. Through an easy flow of accented and non-accented
syllables, stress came at convenient and measured intervals. This
rhythmical effect may be found in the following passage:

The hardy Greeks on the barren shores of Athens and the Spartans
on their sterile plains, built round their freedom and their cities walls
of naked human bodies which all the countless hosts of Xerxes could
not pass. Phillip's mule, with its golden load, entered the gates in
triumph.[10]

Finally, the address was a work of art in its skillful adaptation to
the audience. Comprising the audience were students of Wake
Forest College, a Baptist school, and their parents. Many of the
students were studying for the ministry, and the majority of the
parents were interested in religion. Demonstrating his imagina-

tive powers, Vance designed the following portion of the speech to appeal to these Baptists:

There is doubtless some infidelity among you, as in all other colleges. I know well how it is. When young minds are thoroughly imbued with the Pagan Classics, and come first to exercise their powers of reason, the desire is to test them upon every subject, and especially upon the received creeds of religion, attacking them with almost savage delight. A spell of skepticism comes upon the young senior and the young graduate as naturally as the spell of love ere long — or measles in childhood. . . . He wants the world to know that he, at least, is not to be deluded with cunning devised fables by the Hebrews — Jews! — and old wives tales. It sounds so large to differ with everybody else. It smacks of genius. He is strongly tempted by the glittering fallacies of materialism to forsake the simple faith of his fathers — aye, of his own kind father and anxious mother.

Be not deceived. We all know that 'Reason is but a sorry guide even in the affairs of this world. . . .'[11]

A few years later, on June 20, 1888, Vance delivered a second commencement address at Wake Forest College. This speech marked a definite change in style of presentation. Everyone in the audience waited with expectancy for Vance's wit and humor. They were, however, disappointed. He used no humor, but instead read a scholarly address, word for word, from manuscript. On this occasion Vance used as his subject, *Modern Education and Its Tendencies.*

Evidently, he felt a certain degree of freedom in preparing this speech, for someone connected with the college had written him a letter saying, "Zeb spread yourself. . . . This is a Baptist community, but we are not straight jacketed."[12]

Taking as his theme, "The aim of all education is the exaltation of man and bringing him nearer his creator." Vance presented a speech which had many of the artistic attributes of his earlier Wake Forest address. The entire speech showed thoroughness of preparation, beauty of diction, and grace of style. The editor of the *Biblical Recorder* thought it the ablest address he had ever heard from Senator Vance, but declared it was less popular than the majority of his speeches. This lack of audience appeal may be attributed to Vance's mode of delivery. His reading from manuscript made the speech dull and monotonous.[13]

Perhaps the best of Vance's commemorative speeches was his eulogy on his friend and political guardian, David L. Swain. Because of his close association with President Swain while a student at the university and during his political life afterwards, Vance was considered the person best qualified to perform this important assignment. Preparation of the speech covered a period of more than a year.

At eleven o'clock on June 7, 1877, a procession was formed and Vance was escorted into the Chapel which was crowded with alumni, graduates, and friends, eager to hear the Tarheel spokesman. The building resounded with applause as Vance mounted the platform.[14]

Vance followed a biographical method, organizing the eulogy under the following heads: (1) Swain's ancestry, (2) early life, (3) education, (4) political life, (5) career as university president, (6) ethical and religious traits, (7) death. In simple language he traced the life of his friend from infancy to death, setting forth his virtues and leading traits of character.

Making the eulogy appealing to his audience, Vance used a simple rather than the literary or oratorical style. The sentence structure was less formal than that of most eulogies, and was devoid of ornamentation or embellishment. His sparing use of polysyllabic words also contributed to the effectiveness of the speech. The style was further enhanced by the use of vivid language and a variety of sentence structure. The characteristics of a spoken style may be observed in the introduction to the eulogy:

In this range, about seven miles from where these waters meet, there is a little gorge-like valley scooped out of its western slope, which spreads its narrow bosom precisely in the face of the setting sun. The tall dome of Mt. Mitchell literally casts its shadow over this mountain cradled vale, as the sun first comes up from the Eastern sea.

Great ridges hem it in on either side, gradually melting on the south into the sloping hills on which stands the town of Asheville. A bold fresh brook from springs high up in the mountain, ripples through the bottom of this vale reinforced by hundreds of smaller streams pouring from the ravines on the right and left, and empties its bright fresh floods into the French Broad, five miles below the county seat. Near the head of this valley is a charming little homestead, consisting of fertile bits of meadows on the brook-side, above which are open fields swelling upward to the skies of the mountain forests.[15]

Throughout the address Vance showed excellent judgment in his choice of materials. He gave praise where praise was due, and treated Swain's shortcomings tactfully. His contributions to the progress of the university were enumerated, while his weakness in indulging the students was minimized. Vance explained:

He was utterly incapable of resisting an appeal for mercy, or a tale of distress. This was, I believe, the only objection urged against his conduct on the bench — his leniency to criminals. It was an objection to his honor, if his mercy was at all tempered with discretion, as I doubt not it was. So too arose the only serious trouble he ever had with the trustees of the university.

Stringent measures had been resolved upon by the Boards towards dissipation and insubordination among the students, which regulations were not rigidly enforced by Gov. Swain. So great was his forbearance with the hot blood of youth, and so strong his faith that time would cure these early follies, and enable the better natures of the young men to assert themselves, that he suffered the Draconian code of the Trustees to lie dormant, whilst he lectured, reproved, and exhorted. He shrank from branding the opening years of a young life with sentence of dismission or expulsion, and would condescend to an erring boy while there remained the last hope of reform. In such cases his judgment not unfrequently [*sic*] came into conflict with the opinions of other members of the Faculty, and finally so irritated the Trustees that they passed a resolution of censure upon him.[16]

The yardstick Vance used to measure Swain's greatness was comparison and contrast with great men of other ages. Although

Swain's greatness had not been fully recognized, Vance assured the audience that it would be in due time, as had been the case with many great men of the past. He said:

Modest, and pure and upright, he had the misfortune to live two hundred years before his age, and to put forth fruits of genius which his fellows could not comprehend. . . . Two centuries of progress have brought the world up to where Spinoza died, and it builds him a monument. At last, his work is seen.

The Earl of Murray, Lord Regent of Scotland, was not esteemed a great man in his day. His behavior was modest, his abilities were apparently but moderate, and for more than two hundred years he has figured in History as an ordinary man, overlaid by the more violent and intriguing spirits of his time, and his character obscured and distorted by the glamor which surrounds the name of his beauteous but abandoned sister and murderous Queen Mary. And yet when two centuries afterwards the spirit of Philosophic History comes . . . to show the result of his life's work upon Protestant Christianity . . . we agree . . . that he was in truth one of the best and greatest men. . . .

And so it may be said of Bunyan, of Wesley and of many more whose beginnings were esteemed but of small account, but whose fame has continued to grow continually brighter and brighter, as the world has been forced to see how wisely they builded.[17]

Although praise for Swain was abundant, Vance deserves commendation for avoiding exaggeration. He was not blind to Swain's faults. With tact and good judgment he showed his weaknesses. Speaking of Swain's shortcomings, Vance said:

In many senses of the term Gov. Swain was not a great man. As an author, though a man of letters, he neither achieved nor attempted anything lasting. As a politician, although he rose to the highest honors of his native state, he did not strikingly impress himself upon his times by any great speech, nor by any grand stroke of policy. In this respect he was inferior to many of his contemporaries who constituted, perhaps, the brightest cluster of names in our annals. As a lawyer and a judge, he occupied comparatively about the same position; and as a scholar he was not distinguished, being inferior to several of his co-laborers in the University.[18]

Despite one or two weak spots in the speech, it was sufficiently effective to please the audience. Vance managed to hold interest during most of it, as was shown by the frequent interruptions by applause.[19]

One of the most effective elements of the speech was Vance's delivery. He adapted his voice to the mood of the occasion, as W. J. Peele attests:

I heard Vance deliver his address on Swain ... at the Chapel Hill Commencement of 1877. I well remember the low melancholy and the effortless pathos of his voice.[20]

In addition to eulogies, Vance's occasional speeches included addresses of welcome. Having gained fame as a Southern orator, he was invited to deliver the welcoming address at the International Cotton Exposition in Atlanta, on October 6, 1881. According to Woodward, he extended a "soulful southern welcome" as he invited visitors "to see that we have renewed our youth at the fountains of industry."[21]

Usually speeches of welcome have a single purpose of making the visitors feel at home. Vance's speech, however, had a twofold purpose. He not only tried to make people feel at home, but he also sought to stimulate interest in the progress of the South. The greater emphasis, however, was placed on the second purpose. While extending a cordial welcome to the people of various interests, he aimed at inspiring respect for the South:

To me has been assigned the pleasing duty of welcoming those who come from distant regions to participate in this grand parliament of industry.

We who live by reducing from mother earth the fabric which clothes her children welcome you, men of the West, who following kindred pursuits, live by evolving bread from the fertile-bosom of nature.

You, merchants and shippers of the East and North, we welcome you to this exposition of the productions of a people which assures that they can live and thrive with no other governmental aid than that which is given by peace and respect for the rights of property. ... We invite you with pride to witness these conclusive tests of the genial nature of our climate, the fertility of our soil, the energy of our people, the conservative vitality of our political institutions: in short, we invite you to see that we have renewed our youth at the fountains of industry and found the hills of gold in the energies of an imperishable race.[22]

Appropriate to the occasion, the address was serious, dignified, and relied heavily upon illustrations, allusions, and metaphors for vividness. Vance's skill in imagery was evident in the speech, and it was especially strong in his illustration of the interest of the whole world in cotton. He said:

The merchant in the distant city listens for tidings of its coming up; the manufacturer and his brick walls and tall chimneys anxiously observes its blooms; the restless speculator gazes upon its opening bolls; the mariner, with his broad sails flapping idly against his masts, waits for its maturing — and the poor everywhere pray for the gentle shower and soft sunlight in which it feeds, and rejoice at its safe ingathering.[23]

Vividness and clarity were further enhanced by allusions. Alluding to the scriptures, Vance asked the people of the industrial area to "teach us . . . in all these things a more perfect way." He continued, ". . . We would gladly learn a lesson in industry from the men of the great Northwest, in thrift and art from men of the East; in business and sagacity from the men of the great cities." This allusion was followed by another. In presenting a picture of the South's progress in commerce through the aid of cotton, Vance referred to ancient history. "Through its means," he said, "the splendors of modern commerce are made to surpass the glories of Carthage, of Tyre and of Venice."[24] Obviously this allusion was vivid only to those in the audience who were familiar with the glories of Carthage, Tyre and Venice. Vance, however, assumed that it was in the realm of knowledge of the entire audience, and left his hearers to supply the details.

Vance used figurative language in the address, apparently for clarity and vividness rather than mere adornment. Speaking metaphorically, he said the growth of cotton "is the idyllic poem; it is the melody," and "the king of our commerce."[25]

Fulfilling the requirement of a good conclusion for a welcoming address, Vance placed the speaker and the audience on common ground. This was accomplished through a reference to the death of President Garfield, who had been assassinated less than a month before. He said:

I need not remind you, my countrymen that we stand in the shadow of a great calamity. . . . The sufferings and death of the President of the United States has touched all hearts in this great land. . . . A common sorrow has made every American remember that they have a common country and the cold page of history will say that this reunion of estranged hearts is the noblest monument. . . .

May we not permit the feeling of brotherhood inspired by his death, ever to perish, and may the intermingling here bear fruit in the time to come, with us and with our children, worthy the citizenship of a free Christian Republic.[26]

No study of Vance's occasional speaking would be complete without some consideration of his expository lectures. He delivered so many that all of them cannot be treated in this study, but a sufficient number to acquaint the reader with this phase of his speaking are included.

One of the most significant of Vance's lectures was delivered before the John Andrew Post, No. 15, of the Grand Army of the Republic in Boston in December 8, 1886. The speech, which was one in a series of historical lectures, was titled "The Political and Social Feeling of the South During the War."[27]

The audience was composed of members of the Grand Army of the Republic, who would have normally been antagonistic to a speaker from the South, and the lecture was delivered in an area where people had most strongly opposed the Confederacy.

After being introduced by the mayor of Boston, Vance spoke for two hours, and was frequently interrupted by applause. As the Senator stood before the audience in Tremont Temple, his imposing, portly figure and genial countenance soon won favor.

With his rich, mellow voice he exhibited a powerful and expressive delivery that helped him to gain and hold attention. All the Boston papers reported that the speech had pleased the audience.[28]

The lecture was a plea that the North understand the South. Vance argued that the stigma of treason placed by the North upon all southerners who took part in the war was wrong. "All crime," he said, "is to be found in criminal intent, and no southern man believed he was engaged in rebellion or treason."[29]

Vance's speech in Boston preceded by only a few days that of another southern orator in New York; Henry W. Grady, editor of the *Atlanta Constitution,* presented his "New South" speech on December 22, 1886.[30] Unlike Grady, however, Vance was not conciliatory, appearing almost pugnacious until the conclusion of the speech. He made little effort to adapt to the audience in this respect. The following passage exemplifies the speaker's lack of conciliation:

I believe when you view this thing dispassionately and calmly you will feel bound to give proper credit to both Confederate and State authorities, for their efforts during all the confusion of those unhappy times to preserve both the essence and the forms of personal liberty, under the strongest temptations to disregard them. I feel that it would not be too much in me to say here that we far exceeded your state and certainly your federal government, in these important respects though the strain upon you was not half so hard as on us.[31]

Vance's blunt remarks were softened somewhat by the conclusion of the address. In it he emphasized the fact that the war was not actually fought over slavery, but over constitutional state rights. Appealing to his audience, he expressed a distaste for slavery and a desire that it should never return to the country. With a patriotic flair, he spoke these pleasing sentiments:

My faith is that of those who believe that all human events of nations as of individuals are wisely as well as kindly ordered by the great Ruler of All for the best interests of his creatures, and so that the very wrath of man is made to praise Him. Bitter to my taste as the results of the Civil War were, day after day has reconciled me to them and convinced me of the wisdom of cheerful submission to the will of Him who brought them about. The union of these states has been preserved and declared indissoluble; a great and disturbing constitutional question has been finally settled; and slavery has been forever abolished, no longer to tarnish the fair fame of the great free Republic. Because it was involved in constitutional right, I fought four years in its defence; on the honor of my manhood, I assure you, though my hairs have since become white, that I would fight eight years against the attempt to reinstate it in my country.[32]

Vance's greatest lecture, "The Scattered Nation," was delivered for the first time on February 13, 1874. The number of times the lecture was delivered during the course of his career is only conjecture, but evidence establishes the fact that it was frequently given. It seems certain that over a period of fifteen years "The Scattered Nation" was delivered hundreds of times and in almost every important city in the United States.[33]

Perhaps the curious may wonder why Vance, who lived in a state having only about five hundred Jewish people within its borders, became interested in the Hebrew race. A study of his life reveals some of the reasons. Although Vance was a member of no church until late in life, he had always shown a keen interest in the Bible; this led to an interest in the ancient Hebrew people.

Another factor contributing to Vance's interest in the Jews was his close contact with them. In Statesville prior to his imprisonment, and later in Charlotte after his release, Vance became acquainted with a number of Jewish merchants whose friendship served to inspire "The Scattered Nation."

One of Vance's Jewish friends was Samuel Wittkowsky, who drove Vance to the depot in Salisbury after his arrest by General Hugh Kirkpatrick's cavalry. Wittkowsky became one of the most successful business men in the state.

Vance could not be other than pleased with the contribution his Jewish friends made toward establishing the South's economy. Practically all of them came South with capital, which they placed in circulation by furnishing employment and opening new fields of endeavor. Inspired by his admiration for these men, his study of Hebrew history, and his natural humanitarian spirit, Vance produced one of the most significant lectures of his lifetime.

Vance opened his lecture by comparing the Jewish race with the Gulf Stream. Borrowing a description from Matthew Maury, the famous oceanographer, Vance began as follows:

Says Professor Maury: 'There is a river in the ocean. In the severest droughts it never fails, and in the mightiest floods it never overflows. The Gulf of Mexico is its fountain, and its mouth is in the Arctic seas. It is the Gulf stream. There is in the world no other such majestic flow of waters. Its current is more rapid than the Mississippi or the Amazon, and its volume more than a thousand times greater. Its waters, as far out from the Gulf as the Carolina coasts, are of an indigo blue; they are so distinctly marked that their line of junction with the common sea-water may be traced by the eye. Often one-half of a vessel may be perceived floating in gulf stream water, while the other half is in common water of the sea, so sharp is the line and such want of affinity between those waters, and such too the reluctance, so to speak, on the part of the Gulf Stream to mingle with the common water of the sea.'

This curious phenomenon in the physical world has its counterpart in the moral. There is a lonely river in the midst of the ocean of mankind. The mightiest floods of human temptation have never caused it to overflow and the fiercest fires of human cruelty though seven times heated in the furnace of religious bigotry, have never caused it to dry up, although its waves for two thousand years have rolled crimson with the blood of its martyrs. Its fountain is in the gray dawn of the world's history, and its mouth is somewhere in the shadows of eternity. It too refuses to mingle with the surrounding waves, and the line which divides its restless billows from the common waters of humanity is also plainly visible to the eye. It is the Jewish race.[34]

Since the lecture grew out of Vance's familiarity with the Old Testament and his reading of Jewish history, many of the ideas were, of course, unoriginal. Even the title was lacking in originality, for there had been a missionary periodical called *The Scattered Nation; Past, Present and Future,* published in London in the 1860's. The *Israelite* of March 3, 1871, a Cincinnati Jewish organ, carried an article with the same title.[35]

Vance found the problem of audience adaptation in "The Scattered Nation" different from that of most of his speaking. This may be attributed to the fact that it belonged in the category of the popular lecture. The audiences attending such lectures were usually heterogeneous rather than select. Although specific organizations sponsored the lecture, the general public was encouraged to attend in order to increase the proceeds from admissions. Consequently, the popular lecturer had to choose a subject of wide appeal. While the Jewish problem in itself may have lacked universal appeal, the title of Vance's lecture and the speaker himself were both intriguing. Vance's treatment of the subject made it even more interesting. Attributing the world's progress and civilization to the Jew, Vance expressed his admiration for this remarkable race in these words:

The Jew is beyond doubt the most remarkable man of this world—past or present. Of all the stories of the sons of men, there is none so wild, so wonderful, so full of extreme mutation, so replete with suffering and sorrow, so abounding in extraordinary providences, so overflowing with scenic romance. There is no man who approaches him in the extent and character of the influence which he has exercised over the human family. His history is the history of our civilization and progress in this world, and our faith and hope in that which is to come. From him have we derived the form and pattern of all that is excellent on earth or in heaven. . . . Palestine, his home, was the central chamber of God's administration. He was at once the grand usher to these glorious courts, and repository of the councils of the Almighty and the envoy of the divine mandates to the consciences of men. He was the priest and faith giver to mankind, and as such, in spite of the jibe and jeer, he must ever be considered as occupying a peculiar and sacred relation to all other peoples of this world.[36]

Vance developed the body of the lecture in topical order. He enumerated the main headings before elaborating upon them, thereby enhancing clarity. Promising to glance briefly at the history of the Jews, he divided the body of the address into (1) origin and civilization, (2) present conditions, (3) peculiarities, and (4) probable destiny.[37]

The part of the lecture dealing with the origin and civilization of the Jews consisted of a lengthy quotation from the *American Cyclopedia*.[38] Vance declared that "no people could establish such antiquity of origin, such unbroken generations of descent as the Jews." On this point he took issue with Macaulay's essay on "Rank's History of the Popes." In this essay, Macaulay had said that the line of the Papacy could be traced back farther than any other institution. To this Vance answered that no people could claim such antiquity of origin as the Jewish race — not even Macaulay's popes. Demonstrating an acquaintance with the essay, Vance quoted the following passage:

No other institution is left standing which carries the mind back to the times when smoke of sacrifice rose from the Pantheon, and when camels, leopards, and tigers bounded in the Iberian Amphitheatre.[39]

In developing this first part of the lecture, Vance also emphasized the contributions of the Jews to the rest of the civilized world. First, he said, the Jews gave to the world its monotheistic doctrine.

The second contribution of the Jews to civilization, said Vance, was their commerce. He explained that the Jews were originally engaged in agriculture, but the natural poverty of their country forced them into commerce. Jerusalem, accordingly, became the center of the great caravan routes from the rich countries of the East to the areas around the Mediterranean.[40]

The next most important contribution of the Jews, after religion, thought Vance, was their institutions. Their laws "for the protection of property, the enforcement of industry, and the upholding of the State" contributed to a personal freedom and a national vigor.

The second section of the lecture dwelt with the status of the Jews. Vance explained that many Jews had become merchants, because this seemed the best means of livelihood for an exiled race. By following the great channels of commerce in the world, they found that trading was most adaptable to their needs.

Vance next divided the Jews into three great classes. One class was composed of those who lived in the interior of Africa, Arabia, India, China, Turkestan, and Bokhara. A second, and the most numerous, class inhabited Northern Africa, Egypt, Palestine, Syria, Mesopotamia, Persia, Asia Minor, European Turkey, Poland, Russia, and parts of Austria. This group Vance recognized as ignorant of all but Jewish learning, and consequently adhered strictly to Talmudical Judaism. The third class consisted of those Jews who lived in central and western Europe and the United States. It was with these that the lecture was principally concerned. They were the most intelligent and civilized of their race.[41]

The third division of the lecture was devoted to the Jew's peculiarities. Among other curious facts concerning them, he pointed to their ability to avoid pestilential diseases contracted by their Gentile neighbors, even though they often lived huddled together in crowded and filthy quarters.

Vance considered the Jews' social life the most remarkable of their peculiar features. "There is," he said, "neither prostitution nor pauperism, and but little abject poverty among them."

Many of the peculiarities of the Jews were actually commendable traits of character. Among these were a high regard for education and family life.

The final division of the lecture was concerned with the probable destiny of the Jewish race. Expressing the belief that much progress had been made in dispelling prejudices toward the Jews, Vance said:

There is a morning to open yet for the Jews in Heaven's good time, and if that opening shall be in any way commensurate with the darkness of the night through which they have passed, it will be the brightest ever dawned on a faithful people.[42]

The peroration of the lecture was a continuation of this last division of the body. Using vivid imagery, Vance concluded with an illustration that summarized the high attributes of the Jews and illuminated the prospects of their future. He said:

I have stood on the summit of the very monarch of our Southern Alleghanies and have seen night flee away before the chariot wheels of the God of day. The stars receded before the pillars of fire that pierced the zenith, a thousand ragged mountain peaks began to peer up from the abysmal darkness, each looking through the vapory seas that filled the gorges like an island whose "jutting and confounded base was swilled by the wild and wasteful ocean." As the curtain was lifted more and more and the eastern brightness grew in radiance and in glory, animate nature prepared to receive her Lord; the tiny snow bird from its nest in the turf began chirping to its young; the silver pheasant sounded its morning drum-beat for its mate in the boughs of the fragrant fir, the dun deer rising slowly from his mossy couch and stretching himself in graceful curves, began to crop the tender herbage; whilst the lordly eagle rising straight upward from his home on the crag, with pinions wide spread, bared his golden breast to the yellow beams and screamed his welcome to the sun in his coming! Soon the vapors of the night were lifted upon shafts of fire, rolling and seething in billows of refulgent flame, until, far overhead, they were caught upon the wings of the morning breeze and swept away; perfect day was established and there was peace. So may it be with this long suffering and immortal people. So may the real spirit of Christ yet be triumphantly infused amongst those who profess to obey his teachings, that with one voice and one hand they will stay the persecutions and hush the sorrows of these their wonderous kinsmen, put them forward into the places of honor and the homes of love where all the lands in which they dwell, shall be to them as was Jerusalem to their fathers.[43]

"The Scattered Nation" is considered by many as Vance's best effort. There are several factors responsible for this; but its style is undoubtedly one of the most important reasons for the success of the lecture. Vivid and clear language made it easy to understand. His use of imagery enhanced by apt and unusual quotations from literature aided in holding the audience's interest. Throughout the lecture was demonstrated a highly sensitive imagination in depicting scenes he had never seen. The following passage demonstrates a remarkable imagination stimulated by wide reading:

In the days of Jewish prosperity, it was in all things a fair type of this strange country and people. Enthroned upon the hills of Judah, overflowing with riches, and freewill offerings of a devoted people—decked with the barbaric splendor of eastern taste. It was the rival in power and wonderous beauty of the most magnificent cities of antiquity. Nearly everyone of her great competitors have mouldered into dust. The bat and the owl inhabit their towers, and the fox litters her young in the corridors of their palaces, but Jerusalem still sits in solitary grandeur upon the lonely hills, and though faded, feeble, and ruinous still towers in moral splendor above all the spires and domes and pinnacles ever erected by human hands. . . . I must be content with asking you to imagine what a divine prospect would burst upon the summit of that stately tower; and picture the burning sands of the desert far beyond the mysterious waters of the Dead Sea on the one hand, and the shining waves of the great sea on the other, flecked with white of the Tyrian ships, whilst hoary Lebanon, crowned with its diadem of perpetual snow glittered in the morning light like a dome of fire tempered with the emerald of its cedars—a fillet of glory around its brow.[44]

Another reason why "The Scattered Nation" appealed to people was the freshness of content. The lecture differed from those usually delivered by Vance in that it was a serious effort in its entirety. There was little evidence that it was composed by a man who enjoyed a reputation for drollery.

"The Scattered Nation" gained esteem during the years it was being delivered, and has retained this esteem throughout the years. It has become a part of southern literature.

CHAPTER XI

TARHEEL SPOKESMAN

Following Vance's death in 1894, the people of North Carolina paid a final tribute, manifesting their love and devotion to him. His body was returned from Washington to Raleigh, and was placed in the rotunda of the capitol where hundreds of people came sorrowfully to take their last look at their beloved spokesman. All of North Carolina mourned, and the stations between Raleigh and Asheville were thronged with people as the train carried his body to its final resting place.[1]

The secret of Vance's personal appeal to the people of his native state may be attributed to many factors. His unimpeachable honesty encouraged the people's love. They had learned to rely on his promises and to appreciate his generous nature. During the war he had made a great effort to provide the necessities of life to the soldiers and the people of the state. They were also indebted to him for the maintenance of civil authority and the prevention of illegal arrests. The chief, and probably most significant, factor in his personal hold on the people was, however, his ability to speak.

For almost half a century Vance won the adulation of audiences in all types of speaking situations. Among the several sources of his effectiveness as a speaker was the fact that Vance always had something worth saying. He obtained the material from his own general knowledge and experience. His mind was never idle and he was continually in pursuit of some general information which he could use in his speeches.

Much of his speech material came from his reading, and the influence of Scott, Dickens, and the Bible is often evident. He was

129

a systematic reader; he read by subjects and by periods. This method gave him a reservoir of literary references upon which he could draw.

The fact that Vance always had something to say does not imply that he prepared every speech thoroughly. Although his speeches in the Senate and his lectures were elaborately prepared, his speeches on the hustings were almost entirely impromptu. He claimed that he did his best thinking on his feet, and that his most apt illustrations and arguments were the inspiration of the moment. This feeling was probably based on a favorable audience response rather than a critical judgment of his speaking. According to Thomas L. Clingman, his campaign speeches in the congressional campaign of 1858 carried the crowd because they were so filled with jokes and nonsense. He said, "Vance told so many anecdotes and made so much fun about Know-Nothingism that one-half the crowd thought Avery was the Know-Nothing" even though Vance belonged to the party which bore the name of Know-Nothing.[2]

The process Vance used in the preparation of his more serious speeches consisted of making notes on the subject and writing the speeches in longhand. He would then study the written manuscript and make corrections by inserting new phrases.

Whenever Vance was unable to find appropriate supporting materials for his speeches, he would call upon his own experience, his fertile imagination, or retentive memory to supply him with an apt illustration with which to reinforce his ideas.[3] This creativeness gave his speeches a freshness and originality.

In developing his argumentative and persuasive discourses Vance depended chiefly upon testimony and statistics. These were usually gathered from reliable sources.

Invention as practiced by Vance also included selecting illustrations and figurative expressions that made arguments clear and vivid. One of the best examples of his use of an illustration designed to clarify an argument was made before the Senate on May 6, 1886, in a speech on a bill to regulate commerce. The subject of debate was an amendment prohibiting common carriers from charging a higher rate for carrying freight a hundred miles than for carrying it a thousand miles, as was the case in some sections of the country.

I was down in the lunch-room but a short time ago. I took a sandwich and a glass of milk which was a very short haul. A senator not far from me took a porter house steak and accompaniments. That was a long haul. Now, do you not know that if the keeper of the restaurant had charged me more for the short haul than he did my neighbor for the long haul there would have been a disturbance of the peace in this capitol before many minutes.[4]

Analogies, similies, and metaphors were also used frequently by Vance. A typical example of his use of analogy occurred in his speech before the Senate on March 24, 1886, in which he favored federal aid to education. In opposing the bill for federal aid Senator Hoar of Massachusetts had referred to North Carolina as the "tail state" in education. This remark infuriated Vance who retaliated with an analogy showing the extent of his mortification at Hoar's remarks:

I am much in the condition of a young man of whom I once heard who had the misfortune of being knocked down in a fight with a circus company. Though not much injured, he took to his bed as though he would break his heart, and in reply to those who endeavored to console him by telling him that any man was liable to be knocked down, that there was nothing in that, 'Oh yes,' said he, 'I know that; but, Lord! Lord! they knocked me down with the same stick they stirred the monkeys with.'

It is a source of mortification to me for any Senator to get up and appeal to the figures and say that my state is at the bottom in regard to illiteracy, but it adds a pang to the sharpness of that mortification, it adds another understory to the depth of that humiliation, to be told so by the Senator from the Tewksbury state; a Senator from a state that has fattened on the public taxation of the country; a state that from the very beginning of the foundation of our Government, rather of our struggle for independence, has sacrificed every principle and every profession that was inconvenient for the purpose of gain, to taunt those with poverty who have been kept poor by the process of plunder![5]

The simile is another form of comparison used by Vance. In the same speech on education from which the preceding analogy was cited, Vance vividly used similes to express the belief that the Federal government should aid education as well as provide for the control of a cattle disease in Texas. He said: "The diagnosis of an ailing calf . . . towers over the educational question like jumbo over a narrow-gauge mule or a cedar of Lebanon over a chincapin bush."[6]

As evidence Vance also used specific instances. In his speech on the "Last Days of the War in North Carolina" given before the Maryland Line in Baltimore on February 25, 1885, specific instances served to substantiate his contention that Sherman's army behaved atrociously as it marched from Georgia through North Carolina.

The purely destructive nature of the march was shown by Vance's enumeration of the specific items destroyed at Fayetteville, North Carolina:

He [Sherman] not only burned the arsenal, one of the finest of the United States, . . . but he burned five private dwelling nearby, he burned the principal printing office, that of the old Fayetteville *Observer,* he burned the Old Bank of North Carolina, eleven warehouses, five cotton mills and quite a number of private dwellings in other parts of town, whilst in the suburbs almost a clean sweep was made; in one locality nine houses were burned.[7]

Balance between the logical and emotional did not exist in all of Vance's speeches. In some he became highly emotional and resorted to name calling, or appealed to tradition, humor, or fear. This type of speaking usually occurred before an unlettered mountain audience who came to hear him proclaim his political views in verbose, colorful language. Typical of his emotional speaking was the "Ruffin Barbecue Speech." In discussing the Republican party, he declared, "The Fountain and author of it was Thaddeus Stevens—who has lately gone to his long home—or to Red Sulphur Springs for the summer." Moving quickly from one prejudiced statement to another, he told of the man whom he had met a few days earlier in Lincoln County:

He got up and made a speech—said he abhorred radicalism and was opposed to its tenets—but he meant to vote for Grant and Colfax. He was one of your radical Democrats—a heavenly hell of a fellow, who was entirely opposed to all the doings of hell, but mighty in favor of the devil himself.[8]

By his own admission, Vance appealed to the sense of humor of his mountain audiences. He recalled in his lecture, "The Humorous Side of Politics":

I found very soon that one of the most successful ways of approaching the common people of the mounains was by an appeal to that sense of humor and by an exhibition of entire candor in the expression of opinion and courage in the maintenance thereof.[9]

Vance often used narratives to support his ideas. If he could not recall a suitable story from memory, he would invent one for the occasion. Being well supplied with brief anecdotes, he used them freely. He drew heavily on emotionally-charged narratives, such as the one he used to demonstrate the high degree of enthusiasm that prevailed in his campaign against Settle in 1876. Claiming to have entered Mitchell County believing that the people were three to one against him, he explained that this belief was soon changed by an occurrence along the way. About three miles over the county line Vance and his party stopped at a spring for water. A woman was sitting nearby under an apple tree. She brought them a cup, and seeing him she screamed out, "Great goodness! Ain't that Zeb Vance?" "And then it was," said Vance, "she reversed the order of things as they had it on me in Randolph, and instead of my squeezing a woman's thumbs under the fence, she hugged me."[10]

Closely related to the process of invention is the second division of rhetoric known as disposition, which is concerned with arrangement of the materials gathered in invention and the planning of the speech as a whole. Vance's speeches usually demonstrated a high degree of skill and workmanship in this respect.

Vance's speeches were developed with special attention to the major divisions. His introductions were usually designed to gain attention and to obtain audience rapport. His introductions were usually brief. He spoke for fully two hours in Boston on "The Political and Social South During the War," but his introduction lasted no more than two minutes. Using a brief introduction to gain attention and state his theme, he said:

My presence here tonight, ladies and gentlemen, occasions me a degree of embarrassment. I was prominently involved in the affairs about which I propose to speak, having taken an active part in both the military and civil transactions of my state during the period of the war. On the one hand I am under the duress of your hospitality, which tempts me on the other hand, I somewhat fear that, if I should be too plain spoken, I might become liable to the charge of abusing the privileges of a guest. Should I fail in properly avoiding either extremes, I beg you to give me credit for good intentions at least. I honestly desire to speak the simple truth as it appears to me. This I believe is what you wish to hear! Necessarily my remarks will be discursive and with no pretensions to the preciseness and continuity of narration which should characterize a historical essay. I shall endeavor to entertain you for a brief space with the ideas and observations of occurrences as they appeared to a Southern man concerning the great Civil War.[11]

The content of Vance's speeches often was weak in audience adaptation, but his use of humor usually overcame the difficulty. His humor also removed the sting from the sharp invective and sarcasm which he was prone to use.[12]

Somehow, Vance possessed the ability to combine the humorous and serious material into a unified pattern. A review of Vance's speeches reveals that his prepared speeches usually followed the chronological or topical order of arrangement. His propositions were promoted by main points supported by numerous subordinate points. In his address on the "Last Days of the War in North Carolina" given in Baltimore on February 23, 1885, he used three main heads arranged in chronological order with no less than three subordinate points in each.[13]

The conclusions of Vance's speeches did not conform to any particular pattern. Some were good and others were exceedingly poor. Some appeared to do nothing more than reinforce the goodwill of the audience. Such conclusions were of little value in advancing the purpose of the speech.

Vance made little use of summary conclusions although they would have been beneficial. His longer speeches needed this type of summary to give understanding and a composite view of the speech as a whole. Sometimes his general purpose changed during the course of the speech, and his conclusions did nothing to clarify this situation.

Any weakness in Vance's disposition of materials was overshadowed by his excellence in style. Although Vance was painstaking in his choice of words, his language never appeared studied or labored. His style was marked chiefly by its simplicity, directness, and clarity. He usually chose words that were familiar and vivid enough to hold attention of his audience. Illustrating such a choice of words is this brief passage from a speech delivered in Fayetteville, May 4, 1864:

This is the crisis of our fate. Before the new budding leaves shall have withered and fallen our fate will be decided. This is the time of trial. It is easy to serve one's country in time of peace, and even when this war began and every young man was ready to march, and grey haired men and ladies and boys cheered, it was easy and glorious. . . . The privations of the succeeding three years have brought a need of a different spirit—a brave, pure, unselfish patriotism, willing to act, to suffer and even to die for the country.[14]

For his formal lectures Vance chose less simple words, and used sentences that were more complex. He, however, appeared less florid than many of his contemporaries, and seldom reached the point of ostentation. Audiences attending paid lectures were usually the more enlightened members of a community, who would understand such passages as the following from "The Duties of Defeat":

Perhaps in modern annals there will scarcely be found a parallel to the complete ruin and impoverishment of the people of the Southern States. Absolute annihilation of a great community by armed violence is deemed scarcely possible in modern times, though instances are not wanting among the ancients, before a humane code of international law had interposed to protect the weak against the strong, and mitigate the horrors of war. The most wonderful example was that of Carthage.—Though her walls were twenty-seven miles in circumference, and she should keep five hundred elephants for the public amusements; though she could send three hundred thousand soldiers to the invasion of Greece, . . . yet the iron hand of her rival smote her so utterly in the dust that there is not a vestige left.[15]

At another point in the lecture, his language was designed for an educated audience: "The whole scene reminds one of the portraiture of Rome drawn by one of the panegyrists when addressing the Emperor Theodosius."[16]

Vance's use of vivid language had its drawbacks. He frequently chose words that would have been disapproved by rhetoricians who advocated the use of reputable words. He used many words and idioms that might be classed as vulgarisms. In his "Ruffin Barbecue Speech," he spoke of a "heavenly hell of a fellow," asked "How in the devil is that?" and referred to "shutting his flytrap down on him."[17]

In his campaign against Settle he called the Radicals "the greatest set of striped back and ring-tailed-rascals ever seen."[18] Again in the same campaign, he said, "If we only keep up the good work we'll beat the buggers so bad their mammies won't know them."[19]

Many stories that do not bear repeating in polite society were attributed to Vance. Because of his vulgarity Willam B. Dodd, the southern historian, refused to rate him as a representative of North Carolina civilization. He said of him:

No man in our history has ever been guilty of telling so many filthy stories as he. The larger number of such stories I heard in my youth and which can not be erased from the memory, came from Vance. He tried to teach our people that it was humorous, that it was not harmful to paint every moral with a dirty joke. Even the virtue of his wife made the subject of these stories.[20]

The secret of Vance's success with vulgarity and common language lay in the fact that he knew which audiences would appreciate his stories. Many of his political speeches were attended by crude mountain men who liked his rough and tumble style. Vance needed their votes, so his use of the language of the street became a means to an end.

The soldiers to whom Vance spoke also enjoyed his earthy style. He used language that placed him on their level as he urged them to stay in the fight. Speaking to the soldiers in Virginia, he said:

Boys, if you want peace you must go to the heart of Pennsylvania, and there fight till hell freezes over as hard as a lightwood tree. Boys, you must fight till you fill hell so full of Yankees that their feet will stick out the windows.[21]

A further analysis of Vance's style reveals a fairly orderly composition. He had sufficient variety in sentence patterns to break monotony. The majority of his sentences were consistent with speech style in that they were short. The following sentences from his speech to the graduating class at Wake Forest College show a variety of sentence structure with a predominance of short sentences:

It has long been the opinion of many good and wise men that the tendencies of the northern portion of our people were towards a too absorbed devotion to material development, and that they were fast drifting away from the simple tenets which are the basis of our freedom. But it can no longer be charged upon the North alone. We of the South are fast becoming slaves to the same ideas and pursuits. The great despair which seized us after defeat, the stings of poverty and bitter, bitter humiliation, have brought about this consequence. We hear much said, now, and by those who should know better, about the injudicious agitations of the politicians. People are advised to let politics alone, to seek wealth and develop their country; dig ores from its bosom and build railroads upon its face, and encourage immigration.[22]

Even though his delivery was usually extemporaneous, he sometimes read from manuscript. This was especially true of his later more serious speeches. His effectiveness was somewhat handicapped by this method, because it stifled his spontaneous wit. A busy schedule often forced him to speak impromptu which he did with apparent ease. Of course, his impromptu efforts were often poor in content. This he admitted in a letter to Swain:

I shall have to depend on a compilation of most threadbare platitudes, touching only here and there upon the situation with such boldness as a Roman Senator might display in delivering an oration before Tiberius.[23]

But Vance was at his best when speaking extemporaneously. According to Senator Ransom, he studied and meditated upon the points of his speech until he had mastered them fully.[24] This enabled him to speak fluently and to include or exclude material at will.

There is very little information available on Vance's bodily movements and gestures while speaking. Evidently he used them sparingly. Those who heard him speak said that he never ranted or engaged in stage tricks.[25] According to his own statement, he said that he was speaking, and his hand was "raised in gesture" when the news of the bombardment of Fort Sumter reached him.[26] On accepting the gubernatorial nomination for the third time, he held up both hands in a descriptive gesture as he proclaimed that they had not been stained by dishonest money. Apparently his speeches were enhanced by his facial expression. A reporter for the *Fayetteville Observer* said that while speaking his eyes and manners bespoke the calmness and courage of the trying times in which he lived.[27]

Perhaps the greatest asset of Vance's delivery was his voice, the power of which enabled him to be heard in audiences of any size, and in any type of speaking situation. Although much of his speaking was done in the open air, he was always heard with ease. One critic said that Vance "was a man of force and with all his joyous geniality something of the lion in his makeup."[28] The quality of his voice was extremely pleasant and his tones rich and resonant. These tones, combined with forceful projection, gave it excellent carrying power.

In order to keep pace with his rapid flow of thoughts, Vance spoke with lightning-like speed. His speed, however, did not interfere with comprehension, because his articulation was clear and precise.[29] Vance was expressive when he spoke and was free from any stereotyped patterns. He could easily adapt to the mood of the occasion. Despite the skill with which he manipulated his voice, there was no affectation. He was interested in delivery only as it might serve to give emphasis to the arguments and ideas which he wished to communicate.[30]

Vance's appearance and personality contributed much to the effectiveness of his delivery. The only distracting feature was his right leg which had been shortened by a fall from an apple tree when he was a boy. He wore a high heel on his right shoe, and this gave him an ambling gait as he approached the platform.[31] Before it turned grey, his long raven hair was combed back from his low, broad forehead, and a mustache almost hid his ever present smile.[32]

In spite of the honor and praise heaped on Vance by his native state, imperfections frequently occurred in his speaking. North Carolinians, however, usually viewed these imperfections as assets. When he was poorly prepared for a speech, he could joke his way through it to the satisfaction of his audience. Vance was not a brilliant scholar, but common sense and intuitive judgment prevented this from being an obstacle to his communicating with his audiences, which were composed mostly of rural North Carolinians. His lack of dignity was compensated for by his friendliness. Every

man in the audience, whether rich or poor, felt that Vance was
his friend. So abundant was his humor that he was thought by
some to be a mere jester with a lively mind and a supply of
anecdotes, and nothing more. Indeed, he was well supplied with
jokes, both clean and dirty, but he said himself that he never told
a story in a speech except for a purpose. Often the purpose was to
please a group of rugged mountaineers.

The expression "not without honor save in his own country"
did not apply to Vance. North Carolina honored and revered him
as they had no other person in the history of the state.

Vance's strong devotion to North Carolina prevented his achieving his full potential as a national figure. Selfish for the rights of
his state, he gave a sectional slant to most of his speeches. This
characteristic endeared him more strongly to the people of his
state. In his eulogy on Vance, Senator Ransom said:

> He was of them. He was one of them. He was with them. His
> thoughts, his feelings, his words were theirs. He was their shepherd,
> their champion, their guide, blood of their blood, great, good, noble,
> true, human like they were in all respects, no better, but wiser, abler,
> with higher knowledge and profounder learning.[33]

In spite of the shortcomings in Vance's speeches, he possessed
the capabilities for achieving greatness as a speaker. These capabilities were most adequately summarized by Senator Hoke Smith
of Georgia:

> He was a wonderful orator. With powerful logic, he could array facts
> in simple language, clear and convincing. With a humor and wit never
> equalled, he could delight audiences, while he charmed them with his
> pathos and won them with his logic.[34]

Strength, force, clarity, sincerity, simplicity, humor, power of
argument, and emotional appeal are the qualities that overshadowed Vance's shortcomings. He richly deserved the title of Tarheel
Spokesman.

BIBLIOGRAPHY

Manuscripts

GRAHAM, WILLIAM ALEXANDER. Papers. 15 MS boxes. North Carolina State Department of Archives and History, Raleigh, North Carolina.

GUDGER-LOVE. Papers. Southern Historical Collection, University of North Carolina, Chapel Hill, North Carolina.

HALE, EDWARD JONES. Papers. 3 vols. North Carolina State Department of Archives and History, Raleigh, North Carolina.

SPENCER, MRS. CORNELIA PHILLIPS. Papers. 1859-1905. 2 vols. of mounted papers and 1 MS box. North Carolina State Department of Archives and History, Raleigh, North Carolina.

SWAIN, DAVID LOWRY. Papers. 11 MS boxes. North Carolina State Department of Archives and History, Raleigh, North Carolina.

VANCE, ZEBULON BAIRD. Papers. 18 vols. of mounted papers and 6 MS boxes. North Carolina State Department of Archives and History, Raleigh, North Carolina.

Newspapers

Asheville Citizen, 1881.
Asheville *News,* 1862.
Asheville *Weekly Citizen,* 1858.
Asheville *Weekly News,* 1858.
Atlanta Constitution, 1881.
Beasley's Weekly, 1942.
Biblical Recorder, 1862-1888.
Boston *Globe,* 1886.
Boston Daily Globe, 1886.
Charlotte *Democrat,* 1822-1876.
Charlotte *Observer,* 1873-1941.
Charlotte *Western Democrat,* 1886.
Chicago *Daily News,* 1884.
Der Deutsch Correspondent, 1885.
Fayetteville Observer, 1854-1895.

Fayetteville *Semi-Weekly Observer,* 1860.
Greensboro *Patriot,* 1864.
Milton *Chronicle,* 1868.
New York Times, 1886-1888.
Raleigh *Conservative,* 1864.
Raleigh News, 1876.
Raleigh *News and Observer,* 1886-1916.
Raleigh *Observer,* 1877-1879.
Raleigh Register, 1854-1885.
Raleigh Sentinel, 1866-1877.
Raleigh *Standard,* 1862.
Raleigh *Weekly Confederate,* 1864.
Raleigh *Weekly Conservative,* 1864-1865.
Raleigh *Weekly Standard,* 1862-1864.
Richmond Examiner, 1865.
Richmond Whig, 1865.
Salem People's Free Press, 1862.
Salisbury *Carolina Watchman,* 1876.
Washington *National Intelligencer,* 1858.
Wilmington *Daily Journal,* 1864-1873.

Public Documents, Catalogues, and Pamphlets

ANON. *Sketches of the History of the University of North Carolina and a Catalogue of Officers and Students 1789-1889.*
BATTLE, WILLIAM JAMES, (ed.). *Catalogue of the Dialectic Society, 1795-1890.* Baltimore, 1890.
Catalogue of the University of North Carolina, 1851-1852.
Governor Vance's Record. Raleigh, undated. Copy of source in pamphlet form is in the University of North Carolina Library.
North Carolina. *Legislative Documents.* 1864-1865.
North Carolina. *Public Laws of the State of North Carolina,* 1864-1865.
North Carolina. *Senate House Journals.* 1862-1863.
U. S. *Congressional Globe.* 1858-1861.
U. S. *Congressional Record.* 1879-1893.
War of the Rebellion — Official Record of the Union and Confederate Armies. Vols. XLI-XLVI.

Address by Z. B. Vance Delivered Before the Literary Societies of Wake Forest College, June 26, 1872. Raleigh, 1872.

Ceremonies Attending the Unveiling of the Bronze Statue of Zeb B. Vance. L.L.D. And the Address of Richard H. Battle, L.L.D. Raleigh, 1900.

Life and Character of Hon. David L. Swain by Gov. Zebulon B. Vance. Durham, 1878.

Memorial Addresses on the Life and Character of Zebulon Baird Vance. Washington, 1895.

The Duties of Defeat, An Address by Zebulon Baird Vance. Raleigh, 1866.

The Scattered Nation by Zebulon Baird Vance. New York, 1904.

Books

ALDERMAN, EDWIN ANDERSON and HARRIS, JOEL CHANDLER (eds.). *Library of Southern Literature,* 17 vols. Atlanta, 1907.

ARISTOTLE. *Rhetoric.* Translated by LANE COOPER. New York, 1932.

ARTHUR, JOHN PRESTON. *Western North Carolina, A History.* Raleigh, 1914.

ASHE, SAMUEL A. (ed.). *Biographical History of North Carolina.* 8 vols. Greensboro, 1907.

BALBIRNIE, WILLIAM. *An Account, Historical and Genealogical, from the Earliest Days Till the Present of Vance in Ireland, Vans in Scotland, Anciently Vaux in Scotland and England, and Originally Devaux in France.* Cork, 1860.

BATES, ERNEST SOUTHERLAND. *The Story of Congress.* New York, 1939.

BATTLE, KEMP P. *History of the University of North Carolina.* 2 vols. Raleigh, 1907.

BATTLE, WILLIAM JAMES (ed.). *Memories of An Old Time Tar Heel, Kemp Plummer Battle.* Chapel Hill, 1945.

BRIGANCE, WILLIAM NORWOOD and HOCHMUTH, MARIE KATHRYN (eds.). *A History and Criticism of American Public Address.* 3 vols. New York, 1955.

BRIGANCE, WILLIAM NORWOOD. *Classified Speech Models.* New York, 1930.

The Forms of Address. New York, 1953.

BROOKS, AUBREY LEE and LEFLER, HUGH TALMADGE. *The Papers of Walter Clark.* 2 vols. Chapel Hill, 1948.

CARR, HOWARD B. *The Washington College.* Knoxville, 1935.

CHAMBERLAIN, HOPE SUMMERELL. *Old Days in Chapel Hill.* Chapel Hill, 1926.

CLARK, WALTER (ed.). *North Carolina Regiments 1861-1865.* 5 vols. Goldsboro, 1901.

COLE, ARTHUR CHARLES. *The Whig Party in the South.* Washington, 1913.

CONNER, R. D. W. *North Carolina, Rebuilding An Ancient Commonwealth 1584-1925.* 4 vols. New York, 1929.

COULTER, E. MERTON. *A Short History of Georgia.* Chapel Hill, 1933.

CRAVEN, AVERY O. *The Growth of Southern Nationalism 1848-1861.* Baton Rouge, 1953.

DANIELS, JOSEPHUS. *Editor in Politics.* Chapel Hill, 1941.

DOWD, CLEMENT. *Life of Zebulon B. Vance.* Charlotte, 1897.

FAULKNER, HAROLD UNDERWOOD. *American Economic History,* New York, 1949.

GRANT, U. S. *Personal Memoirs.* 2 vols. New York, 1886.

HAMILTON, J. G. DE ROULHAC. *History of North Carolina.* 4 vols. New York, 1919.

Reconstruction in North Carolina. Raleigh, 1906.

HAMILTON, J. G. DE ROULHAC (ed.). *The Correspondence of Jonathan Worth.* 2 vols. Raleigh, 1909.

HENDERSON, ARCHIBALD. *North Carolina.* 5 vols. *Chicago,* 1941.

The Campus of the First State University. Chapel Hill, 1949.

HENDRICK, BURTON J. *Statesmen of the Lost Cause.* New York, 1939.

HENRY, ROBERT SELPH. *The Story of Reconstruction.* New York, 1951.

HILL, LOUISE BILES. *Joseph E. Brown and the Confederacy.* Chapel Hill, 1939.

HOLDEN, W. W. *Memoirs of W. W. Holden.* 2 vols. Durham, 1911.

LEFLER, HUGH T. *History of North Carolina.* 4 vols. New York, 1956.

LEFLER, HUGH TALMAGE (ed.). *North Carolina History, Told by Contemporaries.* Chapel Hill, 1934.

✓ LEFLER, H. T. and NEWSOME, A. R. *North Carolina: The History of a Southern State.* Chapel Hill, 1954.

MACAULAY, THOMAS BABINGTON. *Critical and Historical Essays by Thomas Babington Macaulay.* 2 vols. London, 1927.

MALONE, DUMAS (ed.). *Dictionary of American Biography.* 20 vols. New York, 1936.

MILTON, GEORGE FORT. *Conflict, The American Civil War.* New York, 1941.

MORISON, S. B. and COMMAGER, H. S. *The Growth of the American Republic.* 2 vols. New York, 1950.

NIVENS, ALLEN. *The Emergence of Lincoln.* 2 vols. New York, 1950.

NORTON, CLARENCE CLIFFORD. *The Democratic Party in North Carolina.* Chapel Hill, 1930.

PEELE, W. J. *Lives of Distinguished North Carolinians.* Raleigh, 1898.

RANDALL, J G. *The Civil War and Reconstruction.* New York, 1937.

REED, THOMAS B. (ed.). *Modern Eloquence.* 10 vols. Philadelphia, 1900.

SHURTER, EDWIN DUBOIS. *Oratory of the South.* New York, 1908.

SIMPKINS, FRANCIS BUTLER. *A History of the South.* New York, 1953.

SPENCER, CORNELIA PHILLIPS. *The Last Ninety Days of the War in North Carolina.* New York, 1886.

STEPHENSON, GEORGE M. *The Political History of the Public Lands from 1840 to 1862.* Boston, 1917.

THONSSEN, LESTER and BAIRD, A. CRAIG. *Speech Criticism: The Development of Standards for Rhetorical Appraisal.* New York, 1939.

WAGSTAFF, HENRY MCGILBERT. *States Rights and Political Parties in North Carolina.* Baltimore, 1906.

WHEELER, JOHN W. *Reminescences and Memoirs of North Carolina.* Columbus, 1884.

WOODWARD, C. VANN. *Origins of the New South, 1877-1913.* Baton Rouge, 1951.

Reunion and Reaction. Boston, 1951.

Unpublished Materials

Diary of DAVID SCHENCK. University of North Carolina Library, 1874.

"Kemp Plummer Battle's Scrapbook of North Carolina History," University of North Carolina, Chapel Hill, North Carolina.

"Stephan B. Weeks' Scrapbook," North Carolina Historical Collection, Chapel Hill, North Carolina.

WOMBLE, IRIS W. "Zebulon Vance: Tar Heel Tribune." Unpublished M.A. thesis, University of Florida, 1949.

Periodicals and Reports

"Address Delivered by Gov. Vance before the Southern Historical Society at White Sulphur Springs, West Virginia, August 18, 1875," *Our Living and Our Dead,* III (July, 1875).

ADLER, SELIG. "Zebulon B. Vance and the 'Scattered Nation.' " *Journal of Southern History,* VII (August, 1941).

Anon. "Political Inconsistency," *North Carolina Historical Review,* III (January, 1926).

BATTLE, K. P. "Biographical Sketch of A. B. Vance," *North Carolina University Magazine,* XIX (March, 1881).

BOYD, WILLIAM K. "North Carolina on the Eve of Secession," *American Historical Association Report,* (Washington, 1910).

HENDRICKS, W. C. "Home of the Vances," *The State,* V (January 22, 1938).

LOGAN, FRENSIE A. "The Legal Status of Public School Education for Negroes in North Carolina: 1877-1894," *North Carolina Historical Review,* XXXII (July, 1955).

JOHNSON, FRONTIS W. "The Courtship of Zeb Vance," *North Carolina Historical Review,* XXXXI (April, 1954).

"Zebulon B. Vance: A Personality Sketch," *North Carolina Historical Review,* XXX (April, 1953).

"Monthly Records of Current Events," *Harper's New Monthly Magazine,* LXXII (December, 1885-May, 1886).

RAPER, HORACE W. "William W. Holden and the Peace Movement in North Carolina," *North Carolina Historical Review,* XXXI (October, 1954).

RATCHFORD, B. U. "The North Carolina Public Debt, 1870-1878," *North Carolina Historical Review,* X (January, 1933).

ROGERS, LOU. "Margaret Baird Vance, A Woman We Should Not Forget," *We the People of North Carolina,* I (January, 1944).

RUSSELL, PHILLIPS. "Hooraw for Vance," *American Mercury,* XXII (February, 1931).

"Summary of the Week's News," *Harper's Magazine,* XIII (January 14, 1886).

WOODWARD, C. VANN. "Bourbonism in Georgia," *North Carolina Historical Review* XVI (January, 1939).

YARBROUGH, MRS. J. A. "Seeing Birthplace of Vance to Be Preserved as A Shrine," *The Uplift,* XXX (August, 1942).

YATES, RICHARD R. "Governor Vance and the Peace Movement," *North Carolina Historical Review,* XVII (April 1940).

"Zebulon B. Vance as War Governor, 1862-1865," *Journal of Southern History,* III (February, 1937).

Personal Interviews

Personal Interviews with Fred Mahler, the grandson of W. W. Holden. May, 1956; August, 1958.

REFERENCES AND NOTES

CHAPTER I

1. Mira Vance to Margaret Davidson, September 14, 1830, Z. B. Vance Papers, State Department of Archives and History, Raleigh.

2. K. P. Battle, "Biographical Sketch of Senator Z. B. Vance," *North Carolina University Magazine*, Old Series, XIX (March, 1881), 257.

3. W. C. Hendricks, "Home of the Vances," *The State*, V (January 22, 1938), 8.

4. William Balbirnie, An Account, *Historical and Genealogical, from the Earliest Days Till the Present of Vance in Ireland, Vans in Scotland, Anciently Vaux in Scotland and England, and Originally DeVaux in France* (Cork, 1860), p. 9.

5. William Vance to Z. B. Vance, London, July 19, 1884, Vance Papers.

6. Hendricks, "Home of the Vances," p. 8.

7. Arthur, *Western North Carolina, A History*, p. 99.

8. Lefler and Newsome, *North Carolina*, p. 235.

9. Unpublished manuscript on "Some Interesting Facts Concerning an Old Family" in "History of the Old Tennent Church," compiled by Reverend Frank Symmes in Gudger-Love Papers. Southern Historical Collection, University of North Carolina, Chapel Hill.

10. Lou Rogers, "Margaret Baird Vance, a Woman We Should Not Forget," *We the People*, January, 1944.

11. Battle, *North Carolina University Magazine*, XIX, 257.

12. Charlotte *Observer*, January 31, 1915.

13. *Ibid.*

14. Arthur, *Western North Carolina, a History*, p. 421.

15. Charlotte *Observer*, January 31, 1915.

16. "Stephan B. Weeks' Scrapbook."

17. Charlotte *Observer*, January 31, 1915.

18. *Address of Richard H. Battle*, p. 11.

19. Iris W. Womble, "Zeb Vance Tar Heel Tribune" (Unpublished M. A. thesis, Department of History, University of Florida, 1949).

20. Charlotte *Observer*, January 31, 1915.

21. Vance to "Cousin Matt," Chapel Hill, August 12, 1851, Vance Papers.

22. Battle, *History of the University of North Carolina*, p. 664.

23. *Catalogue of the University of North Carolina* (1851-1852), p. 31.

24. Dowd, *Life of Vance*, p. 26.

25. Battle, *Catalogue of Dialectic Society*, p. 14.

26. Dowd, *Life of Vance*, p. 15.

27. "Stephan B. Weeks' Scrapbook."

28. *Address of Richard H. Battle*, p. 59.

CHAPTER II

1. Quoted in Lefler and Newsome, *North Carolina*, p. 339.

2. *Address of Richard H. Battle*, p. 15.

3. *Ibid.*

4. Richard E. Yates, "Zebulon B. Vance as War Governor, 1862-1865," *Journal of Southern History*, III (February, 1937), 44.

5. *Dictionary of American Biography*, 21 vols. (New York, 1936), XIX, 158.

6. Vance to "Cousin Kate," Asheville, September 6, 1854, Vance Papers.
7. *Address of Richard H. Battle,* p. 14.
8. Vance to "Cousin Kate," Asheville, September 6, 1854, Vance Papers.
9. Lefler and Newsome, *North Carolina,* pp. 328-329.
10. *Ibid.,* p. 331.
11. Vance to "Cousin Kate," Asheville, September 6, 1854, Vance Papers.
12. Samuel A. Ashe (ed.), *Biographical History of North Carolina* (8 vols.; Greensboro, 1907), VII, p. 479.
13. *Fayetteville Observer,* January 4, 1855.
14. Battle, "Biographical Sketch of Senator Z. B. Vance," p. 258.
15. *Address of Richard H. Battle,* p. 17.
16. *Ibid.,* p. 18.
17. Asheville *Weekly News, July* 8, 1858.
18. *Address of Richard H. Battle,* pp. 17-18.
19. Washington *National Intelligencer,* August 28, 1958.
20. "Kemp Plummer Battle's Scrapbook of North Carolina History," University of North Carolina, Chapel Hill.
21. Dowd, *Life of Vance,* p. 41.
22. Avery O. Craven, *The Growth of Southern Nationalism 1848-1861* (Baton Rouge, 1953), p. 303.
23. *Cong. Globe and Appendix,* 35th Cong., 2 sess., p. 85.
24. *Ibid.*
25. Washington *National Intelligencer,* February 11, 1859.
26. *Ibid.*
27. *Cong. Globe and Appendix,* 35th Cong., 2 sess., p. 86.
28. *Ibid.*
29. *Ibid.*
30. *Ibid.,* p. 87.
31. *Ibid.*
32. *Ibid.*
33. *Ibid.*
34. *Ibid.*
35. Norton, *The Democratic Party in North Carolina,* p. 243.
36. Henry McGilbert Wagstaff, *State Rights and Political Parties in North Carolina 1776-1861* (Baltimore, 1906), pp. 95-96.
37. Burton J. Hendrick, *Statesmen of the Lost Cause* (New York, 1939), p. 345.
38. Dowd, *Life of Vance,* p. 36.
39. *Ibid.,* pp. 36-37.
40. Vance to David Coleman, Asheville, August 29, 1859, Vance Papers.
41. Coleman to Vance, Asheville, August 15, 1859, Vance Papers.
42. Coleman to Vance, Asheville, August 17, 1859, Vance Papers.
43. Vance to Coleman, Asheville, August 29, 1859, Vance Papers.
44. Vance to Coleman, Asheville, August 17, 1859, Vance Papers.
45. I.S.G. Baird to Vance, Asheville, July 9, 1855, Vance Papers.
46. Coleman to Vance, Asheville, August 29, 1859, Vance Papers.
47. Vance to Coleman, Asheville, August 29, 1859, Vance Papers.
48. Battle, "Biographical Sketch of Senator Z. B. Vance," *North Carolina University Magazine,* VI, 227.
49. Norton, *Democratic Party In Ante-Bellum North Carolina 1853-1861,* p. 244.
50. Hendrick, *Statesmen of the Lost Cause,* p. 345.
51. Nevins, *Emergence of Lincoln,* II, 112.
52. *Cong. Globe,* 36th Cong., 1 sess., p. 286.
53. *Ibid.*
54. *Ibid.*
55. *Ibid.*
56. Eaton, *A History of the Old South,* p. 572.
57. *Fayetteville Semi-Weekly Observer,* October 18, 1860.

58. Wagstaff, *State Rights and Political Parties in North Carolina, 1776-1861,* p. 561.

59. Hendrick, *Statesmen of the Lost Cause,* p. 346.

60. *Fayetteville Semi-Weekly Observer,* October 18, 1860.

61. William K. Boyd, "North Carolina on the Eve of Secession," *American Historical Report* (Washington, 1910), p. 177.

62. Hendrick, *Statesmen of the Lost Cause,* p. 345.

63. *Fayetteville Observer,* December 3, 1860.

64. *Ibid.*

65. *Ibid.*

66. Arthur Charles Cole, *The Whig Party in the South* (Washington, 1913), p. 340.

67. *Cong. Globe,* 36th Cong., 2 sess., pp. 363-364.

68. Cole, *The Whig Party in the South,* p. 340.

CHAPTER III

1. Hendrick, *Statesmen of the Lost Cause,* p. 342.

2. Lefler and Newsome, *North Carolina,* p. 426.

3. Cole, *The Whig Party in the South,* p. 340.

4. Richard E. Yates, "Vance as North Carolina War Governor," *Journal of Southern History,* III (February, 1937), p. 45.

5. Holden, *Memoirs of W. W. Holden,* II, 20.

6. Ashe, *History of North Carolina,* II, 716.

7. *Raleigh Register,* July 19, 1862.

8. *Ibid.,* July 23, 1862.

9. Ashe, *History of North Carolina,* II, 717.

10. Lefler and Newsome, *North Carolina,* p. 439.

11. Dowd, *Life of Vance,* p. 69.

12. *Salem People's Free Press,* August 29, 1862.

13. Raleigh *Standard,* August 20, 1862.

14. *Raleigh Register,* August 20, 1862.

15. Raleigh *Weekly Standard,* August 20, 1862.

16. *Ibid.*

17. *Ibid.*

18. *Ibid.*

19. *Ibid.*

20. *Raleigh Register,* September 10, 1862.

21. *Ibid.*

22. *Ibid.*

23. *Ibid.*

24. *Ibid.*

25. *Ibid.*

26. Lefler and Newsome, *North Carolina,* p. 442.

27. *Raleigh Register,* September 10, 1862.

28. *Ibid.*

29. *Ibid.*

30. *Ibid.*

31. *Ibid.*

32. *Ibid.*

33. *Gov. Vance's Record* (Raleigh, Undated), p. 2. (Copy of source in pamphlet form is in the University of North Carolina Library.)

34. Yates, *Journal of Southern History,* III, 55.

35. Walter Clark, ed., *North Carolina Regiments, 1861-65,* 5 vols. (Goldsboro. 1901), III, 321.

36. *Fayetteville Observer,* September 14, 1863.

37. Vance to Jefferson Davis, Raleigh, December 30, 1863, Vance Papers.

38. Davis to Vance, Richmond, January 8, 1864, Vance Papers.
39. Vance to David Swain, Raleigh, January 2, 1864, Vance Papers.
40. Raper, *North Carolina Historical Review*, XXXI, 508.
41. Vance to Swain, Raleigh, January 2, 1864, Vance Papers.
42. Raper, *North Carolina Historical Review*, XXXI, 508.

CHAPTER IV

1. Z. B. Vance to Jefferson Davis, Raleigh, February 9, 1864, in *War of Rebellion: Official Records of the Union and Confederate Armies,* Series I, Vol. LI, Part II, 818.
2. Calvin J. Cowles to Z. B. Vance, Wilkesboro, January 20, 1864.
3. Yates, *North Carolina Historical Review*, XVII, 93.
4. Raleigh *Weekly Conservative*, April 20, 1864.
5. Wilmington *Journal*, May 5, 1864, quoted in Yates, *North Carolina Historical Review*, XVII, 101.
6. Raleigh *Weekly Conservative*, April 20, 1864.
7. *Ibid.*
8. Vance to E. J. Hale, Raleigh, February 11, 1864, E. J. Hale Papers, North Carolina Department of Archives and History, Raleigh.
9. Raleigh *Weekly Conservative*, April 20, 1864.
10. *Ibid.*
11. *Ibid.*
12. *Ibid.*
13. *Ibid.*
14. *Ibid.*
15. J. G. Randall, *The Civil War and Reconstruction,* (New York, 1937), p. 696.
16. Raleigh *Weekly Conservative*, April 20, 1864.
17. Vance to Hale, Raleigh, March 20, 1864, Hale Papers.
18. Raleigh *Weekly Conservative*, April 6, 1864.
19. *Ibid.*
20. *Ibid.*
21. *Ibid.*
22. Ashe, *History of North Carolina*, II, 880.
23. Raleigh *Weekly Standard*, May 18, 1864.
24. Raleigh *Weekly Conservative*, May 4, 1864.
25. *Ibid.*, May 18, 1864.
26. *Ibid.*, June 8, 1864.
27. Wilmington *Daily Journal*, July 22, 1864.
28. Yates, *Journal of Southern History*, III, 72.

CHAPTER V

1. Yates, *North Carolina Historical Review*, XVIII, 315.
2. Vance to D. L. Swain, Raleigh, September 23, 1864.
3. Ibid.
4. J. G. De Roulhac Hamilton, *Reconstruction in North Carolina* (Raleigh, 1906), p. 63.
5. Raleigh *Weekly Conservative*, November 30, 1864.
6. Proclamation of August 24, 1864, Vance Papers.
7. Raleigh *Weekly Conservative*, November 30, 1864.
8. "The Meeting of the Governors," MS, Vance Papers.
9. North Carolina *Legislative Documents*, Sess. 1864-1865, p. 11.
10. *Ibid.*, p. 12.
11. *Ibid.*, p. 17.
12. *Public Laws of the State of North Carolina*, Sess. 1864-1865, pp. 21-22.
13. *Official Records*, Series I, XLII, Part II, 1284.

14. Draft of Second Inaugural Address, December 22, 1864, Vance Papers.
15. *Ibid.*
16. *Ibid.*
17. U. S. Grant, *Personal Memoirs* (2 vols.; New York, 1886), II, 399.
18. Hugh Talmage Lefler (ed.), *North Carolina History, Told by Contemporaries* (Chapel Hill, 1934), p. 310.
19. Ashe, *History of North Carolina,* p. 965.
20. Quoted in Yates, *North Carolina Historical Review,* XVIII, 322.
21. *Ibid.*
22. Raleigh *Weekly Conservative,* March 1, 1865.
23. *Ibid.*
24. *Ibid.*
25. *Ibid.*
26. Vance to Joseph E. Brown, Raleigh, January 18, 1865, printed in *Official Records,* Ser. I, Vol. XLVI, Pt. II, 1093-1094.
27. Raleigh *Weekly Conservative,* March 1, 1865.
28. *Richmond Whig,* February 25, 1865, quoted in *New York Times,* February 28, 1865.
29. *Richmond Examiner,* February 28, 1865, quoted in *New York Times,* March 3, 1865.
30. Yates, *North Carolina Historical Review,* XVIII, 324.
31. Spencer, *The Last Ninety Days of the War in North Carolina,* p. 138.
32. *Ibid.,* p. 134.
33. Vance to Spencer, Statesville, February 17, 1866, Swain Papers.
34. *Ibid.,* Charlotte, April 7, 1866, Swain Papers.
35. Dowd, *Life of Vance,* p. 486.
36. Spencer, *The Last Ninety Days of the War in North Carolina,* p. 184.
37. Vance to Spencer, Statesville, February 17, 1866, Vance Papers.
38. Jonathan Worth to Vance, Raleigh, April 28, 1865, Vance Papers.
39. Yates, *North Carolina Historical Review,* XVIII, 335.
40. Spencer, *The Last Ninety Days of the War in North Carolina,* p. 185.
41. Yates, *North Carolina Historical Review,* XVIII, 337.
42. *Memoirs of W. W. Holden,* II, 47.

CHAPTER VI

1. E. Murray to Vance, Wilmington, March 26, 1866, Vance Papers.
2. Dowd to Vance, Charlotte, February 3, 1866, Vance Papers.
3. *Raleigh Sentinel,* March 23, 1866.
4. Phillips Russell, "Hooraw for Vance," *American Mercury,* XXII (February, 1931), 238.
5. Dowd, *Life of Vance,* p. 106.
6. Diary of David Schenck, November 2, 1874, University of North Carolina Library.
7. *Ibid.*
8. Dowd, *Life of Vance,* p. 117.
9. Vance to Swain, Charlotte, July 26, 1867, Vance Papers.
10. Battle, *History of the University of North Carolina,* p. 754.
11. *The Duties of Defeat, An Address by Zebulon Baird Vance* (Raleigh, 1866), p. 5.
12. *Ibid.,* p. 8.
13. *Ibid.,* p. 10.
14. *Ibid.,* p. 11.
15. *Ibid.,* p. 14.
16. *Ibid.*
17. *Ibid.*
18. *Ibid.,* p. 18.

19. An Executive Order by Andrew Johnson, March 11, 1867, Vance Papers.
20. Dowd, *Life of Vance,* p. 220.
21. "Zebulon B. Vance," *Dictionary of America Biography,* ed. Dumas Malone (20 vols.; New York, 1936) XIX, 161.
22. *Charlotte Democrat,* August 30, 1875.
23. *Raleigh Sentinel,* February 6, 1868.
24. *Ibid.*
25. *Ibid.*
26. *Ibid.,* February 7, 1868.
27. *Ibid.*
28. *Ibid.*
29. *Ibid.,* March 2, 1868.
30. *Ibid.,* March 10, 1868.
31. *Ibid.,* March 16, 1868.
32. *Ibid.,* July 18, 1868.
33. *Ibid.,* November 22, 1870.
34. *Charlotte Democrat,* January 17, 1871.
35. Lefler, *History of North Carolina,* II, 578.
36. *Charlotte Democrat,* February 20, 1872.
37. Hamilton, *Reconstruction in North Carolina,* p. 585.
38. Charlotte *Observer,* August 27, 1873.
39. *Ibid.,* October 22, 1873.
40. *Charlotte Democrat,* November 9, 1874.
41. Lefler, *History of North Carolina,* II, ,82.

CHAPTER VII

1. *Charlotte Democrat,* June 19, 1876.
2. *Ibid.*
3. *Ibid.*
4. *Raleigh Sentinel,* July 8, 1876.
5. *Raleigh Sentinel,* July 14, 1876.
6. Hamilton, *Reconstruction in North Carolina,* p. 649.
7. *Raleigh Sentinel,* July 14, 1876.
8. *Ibid.*
9. *Ibid.,* July 15, 1876.
10. *Ibid.*
11. *Ibid.*
12. *Ibid.*
13. *Ibid.*
14. *Ibid.*
15. *Ibid.*
16. *Ibid.*
17. *Ibid.*
18. Dowd, *Life of Vance,* p. 125.
19. *Raleigh Sentinel,* July 27, 1876.
20. *Ibid.*
21. *Ibid.,* August 9, 1876.
22. *Ibid.,* August 26, 1876.
23. Anon., "Political Inconsistency," *North Carolina Historical Review,* III (January, 1926), 155.
24. Salisbury *Carolina Watchman,* September 7, 1876.
25. *Raleigh Sentinel,* August 12, 1876.
26. *Ibid.*
27. *Ibid.,* October 6, 1876.
28. *Ibid.*
29. *Ibid.,* October 24, 1876.

30. *Ibid.*
31. *Ibid.*, October 29, 1876.
32. *Ibid.*
33. *Ibid.*
34. *Ibid.*
35. *Ibid.*
36. Conner, *North Carolina*, pp. 351-352.
37. Raleigh *Observer, January* 2, 1877.
38. *Ibid.*
39. *Ibid.*
40. Frensie A. Logan, "The Legal Status of Public School Education for Negroes in North Carolina, 1877-1894," *North Carolina Historical Review*, XXXII (July, 1955), 346.
41. Lefler and Newsome, *North Carolina*, p. 472.

CHAPTER VIII

1. Dowd, *Life of Vance*, p. 205.
2. Raleigh *News and Observer*, August 22, 1900.
3. Raleigh *Observer*, January 3, 1877.
4. *Ibid.*
5. *Ibid.*, January 2, 1878.
6. *Ibid.*
7. *Ibid.*, May 21, 1878.
8. *Ibid.*
9. *Ibid.*
10. *Ibid.*
11. *Ibid.*
12. *Ibid.*, July 28, 1878.
13. Lefler and Newsome, *North Carolina*, p. 501.
14. Raleigh *Observer*, July 28, 1878.
15. *Ibid.*
16. *Ibid.*, August 28, 1878.
17. *Ibid.*, January 16, 1879.
18. *Ibid.*, January 29, 1879.

CHAPTER IX

1. Quoted in the Raleigh *Observer*, April 9, 1879.
2. *Cong. Record*, 46th Cong., 1 session, p. 1459.
3. *Ibid.*
4. *Ibid.*
5. *Ibid.*, p. 1460.
6. *Ibid.*, p. 1461.
7. Charlotte *Observer*, February 22, 1881.
8. Raleigh *Observer*, September 4, 1879.
9. S. B. Morison and H. S. Commager, *The Growth of the American Republic* (2 vols.; New York, 1950), II, 222.
10. Bates, *The Story of Congress*, p. 286.
11. *Cong. Record*, 47th Cong., 1 sess., pp. 6460-6461.
12. *Ibid.*
13. *Ibid.*, 47th Cong., 2 sess., p. 2349.
14. "Monthly Record of Current Events," *Harper's New Monthly Magazine*, LXXII (December, 1885-May, 1886), 487.
15. Matthew Josephson, *The Politicos, 1865-1896* (New York, 1938), p. 264.
16. *New York Times*, January 13, 1886.

17. Morison and Commager, *The Growth of the American Republic, 1865-1950,* II, 227.

18. "Summary of the Week's News," *Harper's Magazine,* XLII (January 14, 1886), 24.

19. *New York Times,* January 6, 1886.

20. Chicago *Daily News,* December 11, 1884.

21. *Raleigh Register,* January 28, 1885.

22. *Cong. Record,* 49th Cong., 1 sess., pp. 2945-2946.

23. *Ibid.,* p. 2946.

24. *Ibid.,* p. 2952.

25. *Ibid.,* p. 5851.

26. *Asheville Citizen,* April 3, 1887, copied from the St. Louis *Globe Democrat.*

27. *Cong. Record,* 50th Cong., 1 sess., p. 9293.

28. *Ibid.*

29. *Ibid.,* p. 9294.

30. *Ibid.,* p. 9295.

31. *Ibid.*

32. *Ibid.*

33. *Ibid.*

34. Calvin S. Brice to Vance, New York, September 26, 1888, Vance Papers.

35. *Cong. Record,* 50th Cong., 2 sess., p. 278.

36. *New York Times,* January 15, 1889.

37. Dowd, *Life of Vance,* p. 313.

38. Morison and Commager, *The Growth of the American Republic,* II, 233.

39. Dowd, *Life of Vance,* p. 279.

40. Bates, *The Story of Congress,* p. 305.

41. A. C. Avery to Vance, Morganton, August 12, 1892, Vance Papers.

42. F. M. Simmons to Vance, Raleigh, September 20, 1892, Vance Papers.

43. Thomas W. Strange to Vance, Wilmington, September 24, 1892, Vance Papers.

44. E. J. Hale to Vance, Fayetteville, June 17, 1893, Vance Papers.

45. *Cong. Record,* 53rd Cong. 1 sess., pp. 1125-1131.

46. *Ibid.*

47. *Ibid.*

48. *Ibid.*

49. *Memorial Addresses on the Life and Character of Zebulon Baird Vance,* p. 181.

CHAPTER X

1. Aristotle, *Rhetoric,* trans. Lane Cooper (New York, 1932), 1366a.

2. William Norwood Brigance, *The Forms of Address* (New York, 1953), p. 299.

3. *Address of Ex-Gov. Z. B. Vance Delivered Before the Graduating Class and Literary Societies of Wake Forest College* (Raleigh, 1872), p. 5.

4. *Ibid.*

5. *Ibid.,* p. 6.

6. *Ibid.*

7. *Ibid.,* pp. 13-14.

8. *Ibid.,* pp. 15-16.

9. *Ibid.,* pp. 18-19.

10. *Ibid.*

11. *Ibid.,* p. 30.

12. *Biblical Recorder,* June 20, 1888.

13. *Ibid*

14. Unidentified newspaper clipping, June 17, 1877, in Kemp Battle's "Scrapbook of the University of North Carolina," University of North Carolina Library.

15. *Life and Character of Hon. David L. Swain, Late President of the University of North Carolina — a memorial Oration by Gov. Zebulon B. Vance, Delivered in Gerard Hall on Commencement Day, June 7, 1877* (D u r h a m, 1878), pp. 1-2. Cited hereafter as *Life and Character of David L. Swain.*

16. *Ibid.*, p. 15.
17. *Ibid.*, p. 19.
18. *Ibid.*
19. K. P. Battle's "Scrapbook of the University of North Carolina," p. 28.
20. W. J. Peele, *Lives of Distinguished North Carolinians* (Raleigh, 1898), p. 278.
21. C. Vann Woodward, "Bourbonism in Georgia," *North Carolina Historical Review*, XVI, 1939, 29.
22. *Atlanta Constitution*, October 6, 1881.
23. *Ibid.*
24. *Ibid.*
25. *Ibid.*
26. *Ibid.*
27. Clarence H. Bell to Vance, Boston, July 22, 1886, Vance Papers.
28. *Boston Globe*, December 8, 1886.
29. *Ibid.*
30. William Norwood Brigance, *Classified Speech Models* (New York, 1930), p. 287.
31. *Boston Globe*, December 8, 1886.
32. Dowd, *Life of Vance*, p. 462.
33. "Zebulon B. Vance," *Dictionary of American Biography*, ed. Dumas Malone (20 vols.; New York, 1936), XIX, 161.
34. *The Scattered Nation by Zebulon B. Vance* (New York, 1904), pp. 9-10.
35. Adler, *Journal of Southern History*, VII, 371.
36. *The Scattered Nation by Zebulon B. Vance*, p. 10.
37. *Ibid.*, p. 11.
38. Adler, *Journal of Southern History*, VII, 372.
39. *The Scattered Nation by Zebulon B. Vance*, p. 13. Vance deviated slightly from the original text. In place of Macaulay's phrase, "when camelopards and tigers bounded in the Plavian amphitheatre," Vance said, "when camels, leopards, and tigers bounded in the Iberian amphitheatre." See Rhys, *Critical and Historical Essays by Thomas Babington Macaulay* (2 vols.; London, 1927), II, 38.
40. *Ibid.*, pp. 15-16.
41. *Ibid.*, p. 27.
42. *Ibid.*, p. 40.
43. *Ibid.*
44. *Ibid.*, p. 24.

CHAPTER XI

1. Josephus Daniels, *Editor in Politics* (Chapel Hill, 1941), p. 56.
2. Dowd, *Life of Vance*, p. 120.
3. *Ibid.*, p. 221.
4. *Cong. Record*, 48th Cong., 1 sess., p. 4236.
5. *Ibid.*, p. 2284.
6. *Ibid.*, p. 2209.
7. Dowd, *Life of Vance*, p. 470.
8. Milton *Chronicle*, September 17, 1868.
9. Frontis W. Johnston, "Zebulon B. Vance: a Personality Sketch," *North Carolina Historical Review*, XXX (April, 1953), p. 187.
10. Dowd, *Life of Vance*, p. 154.
11. Boston *Globe*, December 8, 1886.
12. Raleigh *News and Observer*, August 22, 1900.
13. Dowd, *Life of Vance*, pp. 463-493.
14. Raleigh *Conservative*, May 4, 1864.
15. *The Duties of Defeat*, p. 6.
16. *Ibid.*, p. 7.
17. Milton *Chronicle*, September 17, 1868.
18. Raleigh *Sentinel*, October 24, 1876.

19. *Ibid.*
20. Raleigh *News and Observer,* December 17, 1905.
21. Raleigh *Conservative,* May 18, 1864.
22. *Address by Z. B. Vance Delivered Before the Graduating Class and Literary Societies of Wake Forest College, June 26, 1872,* p. 19.
23. Vance to Swain, May 24, 1886, Vance Papers.
24. *Memorial Address on the Life and Character of Zebulon Baird Vance,* p. 28.
25. Charlotte *Observer,* October 12, 1941.
26. Boston *Globe,* December 9, 1886.
27. Fayetteville *Observer,* December 17, 1886.
28. Charlotte *Observer,* October 12, 1941.
29. *Ibid.*
30. Hamitlon, *Reconstruction in North Carolina,* p. 649.
31. Dowd, *Life of Vance,* p. 125.
32. Fayetteville *Observer,* September 12, 1895, quoting Nell W. Ray, a frequent visitor in Vance's home.
33. Dowd, *Life of Vance,* p. 336.
34. Raleigh *News and Observer,* June 23, 1916.

INDEX

157

DATE DUE

AP 19 '78			
OC 3 0 '80			
O8. 2 : ON			
NO 1 3 '80			
NO 1 6 '81			
NO 30			
SE 25 '83			
NO 9 '83			
NOV 8 '84			
NO 2 6 '84			
GAYLORD			PRINTED IN U.S.A.